This Must Be the Place

Reflections on Home

MILTON BRASHER-CUNNINGHAM

Morehouse Publishing
NEW YORK

Unless otherwise noted, the Scripture quotations contained herein are from the New Revised Standard Version Bible, copyright © 1989 by the Division of Christian Education of the National Council of Churches of Christ in the U.S.A. Used by permission. All rights reserved.

Scripture quotations noted CEB are from the Common English Bible, copyright 2011. Used by permission. All rights reserved.

Morehouse Publishing, 19 East 34th Street, New York, NY 10016

Morehouse Publishing is an imprint of Church Publishing Incorporated.

www.churchpublishing.org

Cover image by Jan Urey

Cover design by Laurie Klein Westhafer

Back cover photograph by Mark Branly

Typeset by Denise Hoff

Library of Congress Cataloging-in-Publication Data

Brasher-Cunningham, Milton.

This must be the place: reflections on home / Milton Brasher-Cunningham.

    pages cm

  Includes bibliographical references.

  ISBN 978-0-8192-3209-0 (pbk.)—ISBN 978-0-8192-3210-6 (ebook)
 1. Home—Religious aspects—Christianity. I. Title.

BR115.H56B73 2015

248—dc23

2015022378

Printed in the United States of America

for Ginger—
you are home to me

to the friends and chosen family we have
found in Durham, North Carolina—
the most encouraging city I know

Contents

Acknowledgments

THE IDEA FIRST CAME for this book in one of my stops to talk about *Keeping the Feast: Metaphors for the Meal*. It was hardly unboxed when someone asked, "What are you going to write next?"

"A book about home," I answered. The question was easier to answer than the manuscript was to write. I was able to finish it most of all because of the unfailing encouragement and the editorial prowess of Ginger, my wife. Nancy Bryan at Church Publishing—my official editor—continues to be an encourager, without whom neither book would be a reality. I also want to thank the rooms where I feel like I belong in Durham that created space for me to write: Cocoa Cinnamon, Monuts, Parker and Otis, Fullsteam Brewery, and Old Havana Sandwich Shop. I am grateful for my mother's recollections, both written and recalled, that helped to fill in some details from my childhood.

I don't know why I was surprised to find that a book about home would be one that made me feel vulnerable (hence the phrase "close to home," I guess). Now it seems quite obvious. Going back to the places I remember not only brought back memories, but feelings as well, and gave me the gift of finding some friends I had lost along the way. I found some of myself as well in the things I carried to these pages. To list those who have made me feel at home down through the years would create an encyclopedia of belonging, which would be a book worth writing. For now, I will say thank you with a wider brush. Thank you for making me feel at home.

Peace,

Milton

Introduction

credits

sit long enough in the dark
of the theater, and the credits will
roll down far enough to name
man on corner . . .

who was only on camera for a
moment, or perhaps a line,
moving the tale from here to there
such a man was in my movie today—

he stood in the dark on ninth street
waiting for the light to change;
I drove past and we waved . . .
Well—it was the guy head bob thing

and I came home to find
my wife and stereo schnauzers
ready to play the next scene . . .
he walked out of my story

and on into the night
and the rest of his movie,
of which one credit will say
man in jeep at traffic signal . . .

"**I**T BEGINS like this."

So went the opening sentence to a paragraph of *Bento's Sketchbook* by John Berger,[1] which I was reading in a bookstore café. I didn't get much farther into the chapter because I kept circling that sentence. What begins? What makes a beginning?

Just then a woman began to move into the middle of my curiosity, sliding between the crowded tables to claim the only vacant one available. She was middle-aged (as best I could tell), Asian, a little tired, and quite determined to make sure she got a seat. She carried a large satchel topped with a stack of documents. She pulled out one of the chairs and placed her things on it, then she opened the bag, took out some paper towels, and began to wipe off the table like it was her job, erasing any remnant of those who had sat there before her.

At first I assumed she disinfected out of fear, determined not to be exposed to any lingering germs, but there was not any appearance of anxiety in her movements. The more I watched her (even as I tried not to appear as though I were studying her behavior) I began to see an artist's flair: rather than wiping anything away, she was creating a clean space, laying down a varnish of intention like a layer of paint or polish, preparing the table for this moment when she would sit with her tea and her notebooks in the last light of the afternoon sun.

---

1 John Berger, *Bento's Sketchbook: How Does the Impulse to Draw Something Begin?* (New York: Pantheon Books, 2011), 21.

My eyes moved back and forth between the words on the page and the story she was incarnating at the next table. She had finished her preparation and had seated herself to begin that for which she had come. She reached in the satchel and pulled out a stack of about ten greeting cards, all still in their plastic sheathes, then she carefully opened one of the envelopes, pulled out the card, and laid it on the table. As she turned to sip her tea, the caption caught my eye:

"Thank you for being special."

That's all of the story I was able to follow. It was time to go to work. I wished for the freedom to lean across the chair between us and tell her it had been fascinating to watch her work, but I would have been the only one talking across tables. She had never turned in my direction. She was also not the only story in the room; she was, however, the one I noticed. I marked my place in my book with the receipt from my coffee and made my way out of the store, wondering about the beginning I had seen unfold.

When we were kids, my brother and I used to like to make up stories about people we saw in airports and such. Okay, I liked to make up the stories; Miller was kind enough to listen since we were the only audience each other had during our family travels. My image of who the strangers were leaned toward the fantastic and intriguing. Everyone was a spy or some sort of exotic vagabond. It never crossed my mind to say, "The man in the overcoat is lonely and wishing his daughter would call to see how he is doing," or "The girl in the corner has kept a journal every day for seven years—and it all rhymes."

I keep thinking about the woman and the table and the card and wondering how the story continued. It begins like this: on a winter afternoon, she prepared her heart and her table to make time and room to write inside a card whose front panel read,

"Thank you for being special." Perhaps it was an expression of unflinching gratitude. Maybe they were words that needed to be said to span a breach or mend a wound, but they were not words that came easily, so she had swept the table clean and laid down a layer of love and a blanket of forgiveness in which she could wrap her words and write what she felt rather than what she ought to say. Then again, maybe she was a spy and the whole thing was a brilliant cover.

"It begins like this." When I went back to the book some weeks later to document the page number for the footnote, I found that what I remembered was not what Berger had written. I had my notebook where I had copied the sentence and yet the memory that had given me meaning was not what was actually on the page. His exact words were, "It began like this." In terms of letters, a small thing; in terms of verb tenses, a big change. In terms of memory, an important reminder: none of us remembers what actually happened. We remember what we can, what we carried away, what was handed down, what helps us make meaning.

A couple of months after my first book was published my father asked me if I had a second book in mind. I told him I wanted to write a book about home and he responded, "Based on the way you write on your blog, it sounds like you don't feel like you had a home." There was pain in his voice I wished I could have taken away, yet I had to agree with him to a point. As one who qualifies as a "third culture kid"—born in one culture, raised in another, and not fully belonging to either—home is not easily defined. As my brother often comments, when someone asks where we are from, we have to answer in paragraphs rather than sentences.

I began jotting things down, remembering stories, and talking to my mother, who is our family Keeper of Addresses and Details. She remembers more of my childhood than I do. Many years ago, she wrote a book that told our family's story and gave copies to each of us. Ginger and I were engaged at the time, so Mom welcomed her into the family with her personal copy. One of the things she did was to make a list of all of the addresses where we had lived as a family, and that list became a bit of a road map for my wandering home. I went back to that list and then added the places I had lived since—by myself, with roommates, and with Ginger—and the number of residences broke into the forties.

The list sparked my thinking about what had happened in different places and why each place was different for reasons beyond location. I began to think about choosing eight or ten of them as metaphors for home and the verbs we attach to it: making a home, finding home, leaving home, coming home, stealing home. I began culling the list as I made the emotional and spiritual journey back through memories, both owned and borrowed, and began to discover I was writing a much more autobiographical book than I had imagined. Regardless of the building in which I lived, I was inside, I was coming and going, I was at home.

Who knows what really happened. All we have are the breadcrumbs that seem to find us; they don't show us where to go, only where we have been in ways we could not see when we were making the journey.

"Home" is an essential word in the vocabulary of existence, though not always easily defined. John Berger quotes Novales: "Philosophy is really homesickness."[2] Theology seems much the same. Pick up any novel worth its stuff and someone is leaving

---

2   John Berger, *And Our Faces, My Heart, Brief as Photos* (New York: Vintage International, 1991), 54.

or coming home. The soundtrack of our search for settledness is endless. Whether we have moved our whole lives or stayed in the same place, what home means is a live discussion because a sense of belonging is central to what it means to be human. I've spent the last year curating my collection of stories, re-collecting memories and re-membering the past in ways that illuminate the path from there to me, from then to now, and discovering home is a moveable feast.

When we start talking about home, we often begin with a place: "Where are you from?" The question is simple enough; the answer, however, is not, even for someone whose whole life is lived out in the shadows of the same buildings. As far back as the stories go, we have learned we came from the very dirt we walk on, so there is something to the visceral connections we have to certain places and to the feelings they evoke when we get to them. But what about home? Does that only belong to those whose fortune allowed them to live in a short list of zip codes?

Building a definition of home is much like adding on to a house without a master plan: things just ramble from one room to the next. To talk about home is to talk about place, but it is also to talk about memories, which are real and unreliable at the same time. How it feels to remember an experience is not the same as actually recalling every detail exactly. I look back at pictures of when I was five or fifteen and what I remember about who I was then and what happened is not a well-documented collection of artifacts, but a rather mixed montage of details and feelings, an essence. What we carry with us are the indelible pieces of our experience, which may not even be the biggest events or the most significant moments. What marks our lives are an offhand comment or a passing touch and, in the middle of everything else that seemed important, we are changed.

When I named my blog *Don't Eat Alone*, I added a subtitle: *Thoughts on Food, Faith, Family, and Friends.* Those four words feel central to what home means to me, though I need to find a word for music that begins with F to make the list more complete because there are so many great home songs. At each address I found myself saying, "This must be the place" because at each address I found another piece of what home meant. Home is where we begin, where we find friends, where we leave, where we learn to come back, where we are, and where we are going. Home is where our story gets handed down, where we learn who we are and who we are expected to be, and where we decide what part of those expectations we want to leave on the curb instead of carrying it all off with us. Home is also where we learn what family means and what love looks like. Home is where we find forgiveness and hope, alongside of failure and disappointment; where we learn how people act when they think no one is watching, and how to get through a day; where we unearth the layers of family, the stories and the secrets. We all bear some family resemblance even if we determine not to be them. Home is not about being the sum of our parts, or simply being molded by or responding to our families. Home lies in the creative tension between the two, even as home lies in more than one place.

I have wondered and wandered from house to house and town to town. Each address holds home in its own way, helping to build a definition that continues to grow and change. Whatever direction I may be moving, whether coming or going, I'm on my way home.

CHAPTER 1

Dale Carnegie Drive

snap shot

the little boy standing
in the front yard—
in a single shot of
an unmemorable moment—
is me.
was me.
is me.

who knows why
the picture was taken.
to freeze any frame
of life is to leave
much undeveloped . . .
so look again—

my left foot is lifted:
I am in motion,
going somewhere
beyond the frame,
beginning the journey
between then and now,
from me to me.

WHAT WE REMEMBER about our beginnings is what we have been told: here is where you were born; you were a happy baby; this was our first home; in the beginning God created the heavens and the earth. We shape and share our beginning stories to make some sense of how we got from there to here, individually and collectively. Home is where it all starts.

Bishop Ussher was compelled to nail down a date and time for the start of Creation—Sunday, October 23, 4004 BC—and, in doing so, missed the point of the Genesis account. The storytellers before him who breathed life into the Big Beginning were looking back—after the Exodus, after Moses, after Jacob, after Abraham, after Sarah's laughter, after millennia of meanderings—to tell the story of how it all started. They were not trying to prove or defend anything; they were defining themselves. Some years ago, my wife, Ginger, and I spent the afternoon at the edge of the part of the Grand Canyon that is in the Hualapi Reservation in Nevada, just up the river from the Hoover Dam. We rode out on an old school bus to an unencumbered view of the natural wonder. On the way there, I asked our guide how long the Hualapi had been on that land. "As far back as the stories go," she answered.

When we tell of our beginnings, we go back as far as the stories go. The Genesis account was a way of saying *here is what we have learned so far: there was nothing and then there was something; everything about us comes from Someone—a loving,*

4

imaginative, surprising Source. However we might explain how we began, John Berger says, "Theories of origin are attempts to explain our ongoing relation to the so-evident energy of the universe around us. . . . Every form of interrogation of the stars has been about this, and every theory of origin is a story to describe the experience of being here."[3] Home is where it all starts.

Even to say that in the beginning God was already here is another way of saying we were never alone. Time, as we know it, has a back story, a tale before time. The same is true for our individual lives and our societal roots. There was someone before us who shaped us, prepared for us, and made room for us to be a part of the powerful play that goes on. To try and tell how it all started is to go in a bit of a circle: from where we are, we go back and tell the beginning to carve an arc of meaning back to the present. We spend our lives trying to explain ourselves in order that we might find our place in this world.

Nobody knows how they began until they travel far enough down the road to look back. Genesis was written as an explanation for those returning from exile after they had wandered around for generations. Once they got out of Egypt and began to think of themselves as something other than slaves, they looked back to say, "It began like this." No one beyond those involved knew what happened in Bethlehem until after Jesus was gone. We write from the middle to describe and make sense of our origins so we can make meaning of both the present and the future. I look at the little boy in the picture and then write the story in reverse, looking for my creation story, my nativity. I move ahead by looking back to find where I began.

History, whether public or personal, is rarely an eyewitness account or, at least, an accurate one. We write and tell from

---

3   Berger, *And Our Faces*, 91.

memory—what we re-member (that is, how we put the story back together again) is not as much what happened as it is how we have come to terms with the circumstances, how we have made meaning, what we recall. We remember moments and feelings more than facts. In the earliest chapters of our lives, we remember what we were told, what was handed down. We learn the stories of those that preceded us and those that raised us, and in doing so we begin to learn what love means. What we think home is and what we hope home becomes depend on how those stories are told. The history we construct doesn't use facts for bricks.

Before my beginning, my parents had stories of their own and their parents before them. My family across generations, however, have not been good record keepers. One of my mother's uncles joined the Mormon Church and did a good deal of genealogical work as an expression of his faith, but beyond that none of us has explored much of our family tree. From the time I was small, I can recall my father telling the story of how his mother died in childbirth. He recounted how his father said the doctor offered his parents a choice: Either the mother or the child could live. She chose her son. I was in my thirties and my father in his sixties when the woman I knew as "Grandma C"— his stepmother—gave him a binder full of newspaper clippings and other things about his birth mother that she had saved over the years. From what I could tell, Dad knew nothing of the notebook until that moment. There in the brittle black and white of the aging newsprint was her obituary—she had died almost a month after he was born. After six decades, his creation story changed. How he came to be happened differently than the story he had trusted with his life. I'll never forget the look on his face.

My parents and my birth certificate say I was born in Corpus Christi, Texas, but I had my first birthday on a trek from Texas to New York City, on our way to Africa; my first memory of myself is the picture of me standing in the front yard of our house at 15 Dale Carnegie Road in Bulawayo, Southern Rhodesia. I was about two. I don't remember the photograph being taken, or standing in the yard, or even much of living in Bulawayo. I hold the memory because I have seen this snapshot so many times—the shorts, the striped T-shirt, the white hat, the little sneakers, the one lifted foot—to the point that I feel like every picture I remember of that house on Dale Carnegie Road had me standing in the front yard as though I were some sort of yard art. I've imagined people driving by and thinking, "There's that little boy again. Don't they ever let him go inside?" The moment is so specific it has become timeless: I am always in the yard on Dale Carnegie Road. Milton starts here.

Getting from Texas to Africa as missionaries in 1957 meant first getting to New York and then sailing for thirty-one days around the Cape of Good Hope to Beira, Mozambique. A month or so before wc left, I came down with double pneumonia and had to be hospitalized. When the doctors said it was safe for me to travel, we drove to Oklahoma City to see Grandma C, who was the only family member not living in Texas. While we were there, a man in her church who was a pharmacist told my mother he had a small box of medicine to send to one of our mission hospitals and asked if she would take it, since mailing it would not guarantee it would get there. The box was well packed and had a string handle to make it easy to carry. She took the package, which, she recalls, was an irritation for the rest of the journey.

On board the ship my parents met the Jankes, husband and wife, who lived in Bulawayo and convinced my parents to drive on to their new hometown (we had our car with us) after we docked rather than spend the night in Beira. They knew the way, so we followed them on our first road trip in Africa. We had hardly settled in Bulawayo when I had a relapse of the pneumonia. My mother called Ms. Jankes, who was one of the few people she knew in town, told her what had happened and asked if she knew a pediatrician because I was very ill.

As my mother recalls, Ms. Jankes said, "Put the kettle on. I'm bringing a friend over for tea." Her friend was Dr. Kibble, the only pediatrician in the country. He checked me and said, "Your baby is very ill and I'm very concerned. We don't have the medicine he needs in this country. It is pediatric achromycin. The closest place is Johannesburg and I'm afraid your baby doesn't have that long."

In the midst of his shock, my father mentioned the box they had carried all the way from Oklahoma. Dr. Kibble said, "Let's open it and just see what is in it."

The only thing they found in the box was pediatric achromycin.

I remember the story because it has been told to me again and again, but not before I knew I was named for my father and for his father before him, and not before I remember the picture of me standing in the front yard: Milton in the middle of an endless afternoon, with one foot slightly lifted, ready to step out of the frame.

In 1957 there were few ways to communicate with our family back in the States and none that offered any sort of immediacy. We talked to my grandparents and my aunt and uncle once or twice a year, and then only long enough to pass the phone around and say, "I love you" over and over to the voices trapped in the transatlantic cable. As a result, I didn't grow up with much hands-on sense of my family history. There was one, but I didn't know it. I never lived close enough to go to family reunions, to spend the summers with my grandparents. Only after my parents moved from their home into a smaller apartment did I have much in the way of family heirlooms, and many of those are related to my love of cooking. Ginger and I became the repository for everyone's china, although we never registered for any of our own. We have my maternal grandmother's skillet, my mother's first mixer, and glasses that were wedding gifts to my dad's parents whom I never knew.

I'm not sure I could find any family burial ground other than my father's grave. My one family landmark is the house where my grandparents lived in Texas City, Texas, but none of us has driven by there in years. As far as beginnings go, my known family was my mother and father and, later, my brother. I was almost five the first time I remember seeing my aunt and grandparents, eleven before I truly remember them. Family, as I understood it, was made up of the people in my house, and was not tied to any particular location. I wasn't from anywhere. I was born in Texas and then I left and sailed to Africa so I could end up standing in the front yard at Dale Carnegie Road. And I left there as well.

"Then I left . . ." has been the operative ending to most every chapter of my life. I left Bulawayo, Lusaka, Nairobi, Accra, Houston, Waco, Dallas, Fort Worth, Boston, and Marshfield. Home has never been a place to which I returned because there really wasn't a place to which I go back. Carol Lee Flanders says a culture of belonging is an "intimate connection with the land to which one belongs."[4] Yet for me there was no homestead, no family place, no gathering spot that made me feel rooted. The story of my life has felt more like a series of vignettes than a consistent narrative, or perhaps I should say my consistent narrative was a series of vignettes, a stack of postcards wishing I were

---

4   Quoted in bell hooks, *Belonging: A Culture of Place* (New York: Routledge, 2009), 13.

there. My beginning—my first point of reference—is me standing in the yard. The bemused look on my face seems to ask, "Do I belong here?" The answer I internalized somehow was, "For a time, perhaps." Though I could not find David Carnegie Road again, in the beginning I stood in front of the only house I knew.

The current proliferation of social media has allowed me to reconnect with people I never thought I would encounter again, which has been a gift. Even with those connections, however, I am not good at going back. My life, so far, has not made much of a circle. The beginning feels farther and farther away. In working to understand what the word "home" means, I have made journeys of the heart and mind, but even then all that was left behind has stayed there. What I have learned is that the trails of emotional, spiritual, and relational breadcrumbs we call memories let us return to what is past so we can re-collect what has been scattered, re-construct what is in ruins, and re-member what has been thrown to the edges by the centrifugal force of life. What matters most about my beginning is what I remember: how I put the pieces back together in a way that calls me to be me.

At this writing, I have begun the slide toward sixty and I have lived in five countries and close to a dozen towns and cities. Call me well-traveled. Call me flexible, even versatile. Call me rootless—at least that is what I called myself for most of my life. When we lived in Africa and would prepare to return to the United States on leave every four years, my parents would talk about going "home," but it didn't make sense to me because I was going to a foreign country. I was American by birth, though I did not really know how to be American; I was living in Africa, but I was not African. I was an adult before I learned there was a name for people like me who were born in one culture and grew up in another and did not feel as though they belong in either one. We are third culture kids. From first to twelfth grades, I went to ten different schools. Even the years I stayed in the same place most of my classmates did not; I learned to connect quickly and not to get too attached, to enjoy whatever time there was without much sense of creating either a history or a future.

Home, even for those of us who did not stay put, is the place we come from. It may or may not be where we return, but it is where we begin: our opening scene, though not necessarily our birth; our indelible memory or impression. Before we become, we begin, and that happens at home. Those beginnings offer us a sense of identity, which may or may not reside in our biology, yet home is also about who we come from as much as it is where. Some of us are born one place and find home in another. Home is tied to how we are named and how we name ourselves. I was named Milton. I was named Cunningham. Both names offered something to grow into and something to grow beyond. Home, as the beginning, also has to do with a sense of security and safety. Again, that beginning may not have anything to do with our birth. In *The Sacred Journey: A Memoir of Early Days*, Frederick Buechner talks of life before his father's suicide as "once below a time," using a phrase he borrowed from Dylan Thomas.

> Once below a time, he says in his poem "Fern Hill," meaning, I assume, that, for a child, time in the sense of something to measure and keep track of, time as the great circus parade of past, present, and future, cause and effect, has scarcely started yet and means little because for a child all time is by and large now time and apparently endless.[5]

---

5 Frederick Buechner, *The Sacred Journey: A Memoir of Early Days* (San Francisco: Harper and Row, 1982) 9.

One of the reasons I resonate with so many stories from the Hebrew Scripture is that the people were always moving. Abraham was much older than I when God spoke to him while he was standing in his front yard and he realized that life was about to become a transient exercise. He and Moses and the prophets taught a whole nation of people to stay on the move, to live life on the way rather than at the place. Even Jesus said, "Foxes have dens and the birds in the sky have nests, but the Human One has no place to lay his head" (Luke 9:58, CEB). The story of faith, as I came to understand it, was as rootless as I was. bell hooks says the experience of exile can "change your mind, utterly transform one's perception of the world as home."[6]

Home, for the Hebrew people, was where they had come from and was also a place they had yet to actually reach for much of their story. The land was promised, not actualized. Where they were at any time was probably called home, but it was a moveable feast. Even their image of God and the tabernacle put the Most High in a sort of cosmic Airstream trailer. One day, they would get to the Promised Land, one day they would build the Temple. Once they finally settled down, they were never the same. I wonder how often they went back to all the stones stacked in the desert.

The home of our beginning is also a reference point: this is how life is, or how life is supposed to be. I remember the first time I went to someone else's house for a sleepover and they didn't have a trash can under the sink in the kitchen. The bathroom was not where it was supposed to be. They had different stuff in the fridge. I felt lost, displaced. Home is that place against which everything else is measured. Such a reference point can also be called an altar: the place to where we return to see what

6   hooks, 13.

has changed and how we have changed since the last time. The relational rituals we develop are the spiritual furniture that offers us sanctuary. Herein lies part of the power and pull of liturgy: the well-worn paths of meaning in the prayers and hymns we have sung down the years and the invitation to come once more to the table because all is now ready call us back to our beginnings and send us out on another sojourn. The pulse of God's grace sets the rhythm for remembering and becoming.

In Robert Olen Butler's short story "Fairy Tale," the narrator, a Vietnamese immigrant new to both the American land and its language, connects a soldier's account of climbing up on a bull to ride it with the "once upon a time" beginnings of children's stories and asks another man if they mean the same thing. He says they do. "I think this is very nice," she says, "how you get up on the back of time and ride and you don't know where it will go and when it will throw you off."[7] By the time I became yard art, I had sailed ten thousand miles and nearly died. Twice. Yet, for all I knew, I was home. That was my yard, my house. I don't remember much of Rhodesia at all and, somehow, I look into that little boy's eyes and see me. I feel like this is where I began, where I climbed up on a time to tell the story of Milton. It began like this . . . .

---

7 Robert Olen Butler, "Fairy Tale," in *A Good Scent from a Strange Mountain* (New York: Grove Press, 1992), 45.

CHAPTER 2

Valentine Close

calling

when the little dog found us
at the farmers' market
they said her name was Dixie,
but she didn't answer

for the first few days we tried
on several new names
as if we were solving a
puzzle, breaking a code

when we called her Lila
she tilted her head in
recognition: that's me;
you finally found my name

at twelve, my nephew changed his
name, wanting to be called
something other than the first
name he had been given

called by name like a prophet,
named by the resonance
and rhythm of the Spirit . . .
who am I called to be

I'VE LIVED on three dead-end streets in my life, one of which was a dead-end, one-way street—but we will get to that later. The first was in Lusaka, Zambia, where the street was referred to as a close rather than a cul-de-sac: Valentine Close—the name carries its own story. One of the built-in surprises of the English language is that how a word is pronounced is not necessarily evident just by looking at it. To think of a street that is an end unto itself might lead one to think it would be pronounced in the same way you would close a door, or a window, or a book. No. It was pronounced close, as in near to one another, next to, up against. A close is the end of the road. The destination or at least the end of this part of the journey. Go no further, or turn around. A regular street always has some possibility of passing through on your way to somewhere; a close shuts the whole thing down: turn around; try again; don't sit here at the dead end; turn around and go out into the world. Valentine Close. Somewhere in Zambia there was a poet who named streets.

I remember a single-story house, concrete block with a stucco finish, that sat up higher than the street. The dirt driveway climbed up to the house and then turned to create a couple of parking places. There was a large tree to the left of the house, but little else in terms of vegetation other than a grassy yard that was either green or brown depending on whether or not it was the rainy season. The front door opened into a small entryway with the living room to the right, which then circled into the dining room, through a door into the kitchen, and then a small door that came back to the entryway and the hall that led to the bedrooms. My brother and I shared a room, complete with bunk beds and a giant chest full of all kinds of sports equipment and stuffed animals, the prop department for the theater of our lives. We were young together in this house, not yet to an age where we went out on adventures of our own.

The mission house sat on the corner of the close and a main city thoroughfare, Ridgeway Avenue, so it was a mix of traffic and tranquility. I don't remember doing much at the quiet end of the street. Our lives aimed toward the city, and particularly Matero Township, where my parents helped start a church, and Lusaka Infants' School, where I began a life of learning in earnest. The school housed only first and second grade as a way of getting everyone off to a good start. I was one of only a couple of Americans. Most of the students were Zambian nationals or European expatriates. I learned quickly to imitate the accents of those around me without realizing that was what I was doing. When my mother came to school for a parent-teacher meeting, my teacher said, "I didn't know Milton's father was married to an American." When my mother told her we were all Americans, she replied, "Based on Milton's accent I had already decided what part of England you called home." My mother had no idea because I sounded like her when I was at our house. Without realizing it, I had learned to adapt, to fit in, to become part of those around me. Part of what I learned was I was the only kid I knew named Milton.

Besides learning to answer to it, the first thing I remember learning about my name was that it was a hand-me-down; it had belonged to both my grandfather and my dad; I was Milton III. The name is unusual. I was almost a teenager before I remember meeting someone named Milton who was not related to me, so my experience in school was different from some of my classmates who shared names with others in the room; that didn't happen to me until I was with my family.

My grandfather died before I was born. All I knew of him was what I saw in a few pictures and what I learned in even fewer stories. He was a big man in both size and spirit, unabashed in his anger, passion, and evangelism. He was also a man deeply acquainted with grief. His first wife, Bertha, died about a month after my father was born. Milton the First struggled to raise a son on his own. He was a Christian soldier determined to fight the good fight. Still, for me he was the stuff of legend and cautionary tales. My father was my point of reference for who a Milton was and what a Milton did.

Milton the Second was both a reflection of and a reaction to his namesake. Physically, my dad never measured up to his father. He was about five inches shorter. As he grew up, my dad resisted the mantle of ministry handed down by his father. He was a motherless child who often felt fatherless as well, as his dad went west to start churches in Arizona and California. He was an only child who spent his life in search of a blessing his father could not offer. Milton the Elder dropped dead of a heart attack at age fifty-seven, when my father was in his mid-twenties, leaving much between them that had yet to be worked out. My dad aimed his life out into the world, determined to find the blessing his father could not give him.

One of the challenges of living with someone who shared my name was figuring out what to call one another. Since Dad already had dibs on Milton and had an aversion to nicknames like Junior and Trey, I became "Milton E.," borrowing the first letter from our middle name to create my moniker. I tired of it by the time I was out of elementary school because it felt diminutive and diminishing, and I didn't like my middle name, but it stayed with me for many years. When I was at school, I was fortunate to be the only one in my class with my name. I didn't have to share it. When I came home, I had to take both a number and a letter to put me in my place.

Thus I began to learn how to become Milton in a house that already had one; I assumed I was to be like him. When I was in second grade, my mother gave me a copy of *When We Were Very Young* by A. A. Milne. Growing up in a British educational culture meant I was well acquainted with Winnie the Pooh and Paddington Bear. Milne's poetry fit right in. She gave me the book primarily because my father had learned one of the poems when he was in second grade and Mom thought it would be fun for me to learn the same one and perform it for him. The poem was "Missing," which begins, "Has anybody seen my mouse?" I remember standing in front of him and reciting it, how he smiled and laughed and told me about his life in second grade. He was Milton. So was I. Home, I began to realize, was where we come to terms with the people who named us.

Becoming my version of Milton meant I learned that I loved to sing and act even as I learned to accept that I was an amazingly average athlete. My father saw sports as the ultimate metaphor. It was in the throes of athletic competition that one learned to win and to lose, to persevere, to work as a team. He loved any kind of sporting event and he wanted us to play whatever we could. Had we grown up in the organized structure that is American school sports, I'm sure I would have played something every season. Playing sports was where you learned a lot of life's lessons with less pain, he told us. Perhaps he was right. As one who was never fastest or first picked, I learned how to sit on a bench and how to share in the success of others. I also learned how to lose, which was an important lesson, and I learned it over and over. I learned that sometimes you get to win as well. I also learned that life isn't always like sports. Even if it is how we play the game and not whether we win or lose, our existence cannot be reduced to a competition. Well, it can, but then we end up with the kind of ridiculous discourse that spews daily out of our pundits and politicians sizing up the winners and losers of the issue du jour. When life is measured by victories, we become consumed with conquest.

To be a success in sports means you have to win. After all of the great games and touching stories, after all the buzzer beaters and overtime thrillers, what is mostly remembered is who won. That's the seminal lesson of sports, or at least it is the one I most internalized. Life, however, is not a winner-take-all competition. I do think of it as a team sport. Yes, there are those who keep score, who consider who is winning, and who fouled without getting called for it. But here's the way the writer of Hebrews talks about it:

> Therefore, since we are surrounded by so great a cloud of witnesses, let us lay aside every weight and the sin that clings so closely, and let us run with perseverance the race that is set before us, looking to Jesus the pioneer and perfector of our faith, who for the sake of the joy that was set before him endured the cross, disregarding its shame, and has taken his seat at the right hand of the throne of God. (Hebrews 12:1)

My brother, Miller, was the natural athlete. I was a born benchwarmer. I played on teams because I was Milton, my father's son, and I also signed up for plays and musicals because I was becoming me. What I didn't find out until much later in my life was that my father grew up singing as well. When he was a young boy, he would often sing before his father preached. When he decided to become a preacher, he also decided he couldn't do both, so he quit singing, other than singing hymns around the house, which were my lullabies as a baby. We were more alike than I knew.

On Valentine Close I started school, learned how to read and write in English, learned to speak in English and Syndabele, rode my first bicycle, started cooking with my mother, and began figuring out what it meant to be Milton III, which also meant figuring out how to live with the others in the house. Home is where we first learn how to be ourselves within a family. My brother and I had to learn how to be sons and brothers; my parents were learning how to be mother and father. I don't have much of an idea of what it felt like for my parents to raise their sons so far away from our relatives and in a place that bore such little resemblance to how they had been raised. My mother spent her whole life in Texas City, Texas. Dad graduated from high school in Austin. Life, for both of them, had been in the Lone Star State, and now they were raising their children on a dead-end street in Africa. If they were anxious about it, they never let my brother and me know. They did let us know they felt called to be there. Life, as it was presented to us, was an adventure, and I was named after two men who were determined to live out loud. Home is where we are named. When the English speak of a person, they say, "I met a woman called Karen," where we Americans say, "I met a woman named Karen." If I am called by my name, it doesn't feel like much of a theological stretch to say I am called to be me. Home is where I am called by my name, and then invited to step into life, face the world, and see who I can become.

CHAPTER 3

Harding Road

percussion

love is the drum
that beats in our bones
even in our broken
melodies of grief
our symphonies of
sorrow and sadness
relentless resonance
in the late night club
of all that could have been
the hope of the high hat
the syncopation of surprise
the gentle jazz of joy
put your hands together
love is the drum

Our lives may be determined less by our childhood
than by the way we have learned to imagine our
childhoods."

—James Hillman, *The Soul's Code*

ONE OF THE EXPERIENCES of family that was new to me
in getting married was finding out what it was like to
be around extended family—uncles, aunts, and cousins.
Both of Ginger's parents had multiple siblings, and they all had
children. Though she was an only child, she grew up with a wide
community of relatives who lived nearby and who came by often.
My father was an only child. My mother had one sister who had
two children. Even if we had all lived on the same side of the
Atlantic, we could have had our family reunions in a minivan. I
did get a taste of an extended family, however, when we moved
across town in Lusaka to Harding Road.

Our house sat in the middle of the block. A large brick wall
served to separate it from the street, with a gate into a gravel
driveway that led to a carport, which opened up on a brick patio
and what I remember as a large backyard bordered by a wire
mesh fence. The mission had built the home for us, so we had
had some say in how it was laid out, but we had not lived there
long before we realized the best feature of the house was not
something we had planned: the family next door. The Geaches
were a white family with roots in what was then Southern
Rhodesia; they had moved north for Mr. Geach's job. They had

four sons and my brother, Miller, and I fell right in the middle of them age-wise. An African family who lived on their property and worked for them had three children, also our age. On the other side of the Geaches was an Afrikaans family who had a daughter, the oldest of our group, who could hit a baseball farther than any of us. I can still see my father's delight at her clearing the back fence with a home run ball, which sent somebody over the back fence to search for it in the vacant lot behind us. We were our neighborhood family.

Both Mr. and Ms. Geach worked during the day, so my mother became the stay-at-home parent for the whole street. She made cookies, fried doughnuts, and played chauffeur when needed. Within a couple of weeks, Mr. Geach installed a gate between the two backyards to keep us from breaking the fence as we jumped from yard to yard. Afternoons in our backyards were festivals of imagination. Whatever was going on in the world happened at our place as well. When big soccer games were being played internationally, we played them out on our pitch. When cricket was in the news, we had a test match of our own. When the annual Military Tattoo—a theatrical display of the army's training and abilities—took place at City Stadium in Lusaka, we acted out our own version, marching and singing in and out of our homemade fort. After we saw the movie *Tokyo Olympiad*, which chronicled the 1964 Games, we put on an Olympics of our own with events from wrestling to a "marathon" that sent us running through our neighborhood streets.

The other extended family was at Matero Baptist Church, where my parents were assigned to work. It was located in one of the townships of Lusaka, which meant one of the poorer neighborhoods. Soon after we arrived there, the church called Lazarus Green as pastor. The Greens, Lazarus and Rebecca, had five children; once again, my brother and I fell in the middle of the mix. The two oldest brothers, Wynnegood and Norman, loved to sing and the four of us made music together. Sundays at Matero meant lots of singing. The church had no instruments for economic reasons, not theological ones. We were undaunted. Rebecca would start a song and the congregation would join in with harmonies, clapping in various rhythms to add the percussion. The cinder-block building had a concrete floor and a tin roof, so the sounds we made bounced off the walls and filled the room with our joyful noise. We would sing our way into church and then sing our way out when it was over, still making music as we spilled out of the building and into the township. Whether at church or in our backyard, joy was our common currency.

Bill Holm, who grew up in a small town in Minnesota, talks about what childhood, at its best, should offer a child:

> Most important, we inherit the interior confidence that the universe is a safe house for us. That if we don't close ourselves away through fear, the currents of simple love, kindness, civility, will find us out, feed us cookies, and tuck us in.[8]

Living on Harding Road taught me that home was a launching pad, a touchstone from which I moved out into the neighborhood and into the world. "The LORD will keep your going out and your coming in from this time on and forevermore," wrote the psalmist (121:8). Granted, I was an extrovert born into a family of extroverts: we were all outward facing in our orientation to life, so we all went out and, more times than not, brought someone else home with us.

---

8   Bill Holm, *The Heart Can Be Filled Anywhere on Earth* (Minneapolis, MN: Milkweed Editions, 2001), 110.

While we lived on Harding Road, I was a charter student at the Lusaka International School. When the school opened offering grades one through six, there were forty students from twenty-two countries. My fourth grade teacher was Ms. Reedy, who knew a thing or two about joy herself. She showed up one day with a copy of Madeleine L'Engle's *A Wrinkle in Time* and told us she would read from it at the end of the day if we finished our work early. We surprised her with our work ethic because we loved the story so much. The book grabbed me in those days and has never let go. The next two books in the series came out when I was in high school, the fourth my senior year in college, and the last two in the late eighties. I've read them all more than once, but I still keep coming back to the one we first read together.

About the time the fourth book came out, I sat down one day and wrote the author a letter that began something like, "Dear Madeleine, you've been my friend for a long time even though we have never met." I told her about Ms. Reedy and all that her writing had meant to me and I sent it to Farrar, Strauss, and Giroux—L'Engle's publisher—without much expectation of it ever finding her. A month or so later, I got a handwritten response that sounded like a letter from an old friend. We wrote back and forth for a short while. When her husband, Hugh, died, I received a form letter that marked his passing and that was the last time we corresponded. Even in that letter, I learned from her; her first sentence was my introduction to the power of keeping time by the liturgical year: "He got sick just after Epiphany," she said, "and he was gone by Pentecost." Instead of saying "He got sick in January and died in May," her words were full of holy and heavier things. She was also someone who relished belonging to an untamed God. She was once asked, "So to you faith is not a comfort?"

She answered, "Good heavens, no. It's a challenge: I dare you to believe in God. I dare you to think [our existence] wasn't an accident."

Earlier this year her granddaughter Charlotte published three pages that were left out of *A Wrinkle in Time* because they were seen as too overtly political. This excerpt reminded me of the mark Madeleine left on my life:

> "Well—but I want to be secure, Father. I *hate* feeling insecure."
>
> "But you don't love security enough so that you guide your life by it, Meg. You weren't thinking of security when you came to rescue me with Mrs. Who, Mrs. Whatsit, and Mrs. Which." . . .
>
> "I've come to the conclusion," Mr. Murray said slowly, "that it's the greatest evil there is. Suppose your great grandmother, and all those like her, had worried about security? They'd never have gone across the land in flimsy covered wagons. Our country has been greatest when it has been most insecure. This sick longing for security is a dangerous thing, Meg."[9]

In those days on Harding Road I learned to live in joy, to trust that sadness or difficulty or failure were never the last words. The people at Matero who filled up the room with song were acquainted with grief; they were not naive. Life was hard and God was faithful. Both things were true and they chose to sing

---

9 https://s3.amazonaws.com/s3.documentcloud.org/documents/1881486/a-wrinkle-in-time-excerpt.pdf.

about the latter. One of the prayers from the Book of Common Prayer attributed to Augustine reads:

> Keep watch, dear Lord, with those who work, or watch, or weep this night, and give your angels charge over those who sleep. Tend the sick, Lord Christ; give rest to the weary, bless the dying, soothe the suffering, pity the afflicted, shield the joyous; and all for your love's sake.[10]

Shield the joyous. All the recipients are vulnerable and fragile. In Augustine's mind, the joyous were no different. Joy was fragile: The joyous would need protection. When I look back on Harding Road, both L'Engle's caution against security and Augustine's prayer for shielding both make sense. We were not taught to play it safe; we were taught to play with all our hearts, and we came in at night with our share of cuts and bruises, alongside of the memories we made. We also knew we were protected, we were shielded, as the old hymn says, leaning on the everlasting arms.

---

10 *The Book of Common Prayer* (New York: The Church Hymnal Corporation, 1979), 134.

CHAPTER 4

Mwitu Estates

evensong

when darkness falls outside
and inside at the end
of a pretty good day
I've turned on the music
I know—songs that have
lighted many nights with
the spark of steel strings
fingers picking a pattern
of hope and friendship
as comforting as the wind

as old as my high school
afternoons spent sitting
in the grass trying to make
my fingers move like his
I would put down my guitar
and sing harmony while he
sang ain't it good to know
and I knew he was telling
the truth, like he is tonight

I bought that record
in ninth grade—forty-five
years ago—Nairobi days
when I was still learning
how to play guitar, how to
be a friend, how to be me;
the decades have drawn
new lines and old ones—
I still can't play like him
and I can sing the harmony

D URING THE TIME we lived in Africa, the city where I lived longest was Lusaka, Zambia. The one to which I feel most connected, however, is Nairobi, Kenya. We moved so my father had access to a better airport. We found a house about twelve miles from the city center in a little community called Karen, named after Karen Blixen (Isak Denisen) who wrote *Out of Africa* and *Babette's Feast*. Our house was built on land that had once been part of her farm. The people on our circular street, called Mwitu Estates, included goat farmers, a strawberry farmer, diplomats, and members of the Leakey family who were a part of some of the essential anthropological discoveries in Africa.

We only lived there for two years. Part of the strong connection to Nairobi was because of my age: I was in eighth and ninth grade during the years there. Kenya in the late sixties and early seventies was almost idyllic. As teenagers, my brother, our friends, and I hitchhiked into town on Saturday mornings to spend the day in the city. We were picked up by diplomatic limos, crowded buses, and trucks filled with pigs and chickens. We knew we were safe. We felt like it was our town. Part of the connection was our house, a wonderful open home on six acres of landscaped property—lawns and rose gardens and a little bit of woods—with room for everything from a volleyball court to a go-kart track. A big part of it was the variety of people who came through our lives. If being at home on Harding Road meant family extended to friends and neighbors, then home in Mwitu Estates connected me to an even larger community.

During our first year in Nairobi, Miller and I both went to Rossalyn Academy, a Mennonite school where most of the other missionary kids attended. The school was housed in the center of a coffee plantation. The coffee was still there, but the growers didn't use the buildings any more. The school went through eighth grade. When I started high school, my parents enrolled me in Nairobi International School (NIS), which was where most of the American kids attended, along with a variety of students from Kenya and around the world. It was in the middle of another coffee farm. All of the other MKs, however, went to boarding school at Rift Valley Academy, which was about an hour away. Mom and Dad didn't want to send us to boarding school when there was a good school in town, so I became the first and only missionary kid at NIS. It was a world of wider faith perspectives than just mine. I found friends who did not go to church, who practiced different faiths, and were people just like me. I loved being there.

Mwitu was also where I got my first guitar. When I was in second grade, my parents decided it was time for me to take piano lessons. I went through several teachers over the next year and a half. One day after a lesson the instructor came out to the car and implored my mother to let me quit. "He has musical ability and he will find it," she said. "Just not now. If you make him keep coming, he and I will both hate music before it's over." Christmas morning of 1969 my brother and I came down to find cards on the tree bearing our names. Each of the cards was attached to strings draped all across the room. At the end of the strings we found our guitars.

My parents hired a man to come and give us lessons. My singular memory of those lessons was his trying to teach me how to play a song called "Old Black Joe." He had about as much luck as my piano instructor. I learned to play guitar from my friends at school who were all better than I was and had had their guitars longer. We took them to school with us and during lunch and whenever we had a chance we sat in the grass in the middle of the small cluster of buildings and played folk and protest songs. One of our teachers offered to give us a music credit for what we were already doing if we were willing to organize ourselves into what became known as Folk Group. We jumped at the chance. We learned everything from Joan Baez and Dylan to the Mamas and Papas to Crosby, Stills, and Nash. I learned to play chords and finger pick. I learned to sing harmony. I learned how to be a part of a group.

During my ninth grade year my father traveled a great deal. Out of fifty-two weeks he was gone thirty-six. He visited so many countries that he had three extension packs of pages to his passport. We had moved to Nairobi for him to chase his dream of using radio and television as a way to reach the continent and change the paradigm of mission work. Instead of a missionary being the one in charge, a Zambian could go with a battery-operated cassette player and a stack of tapes to start a church in remote places. He turned a little garage-like building on our property into a makeshift dubbing room and paid me to dub tapes for him after school. In his way, he helped to start churches he never saw.

Wherever we lived while my parents were missionaries, they drew a wide circle of inclusion. The parade of people through our house was varied and vibrant. What I internalized from watching them was that the point was not to go and tell people as much as it was to go and be with them. They looked for ways to include and to be included.

The American community in Nairobi was substantial. As we settled into our house, my parents came up with the idea of what became known as Play Day. Any time there was a fifth Saturday in a month, we invited whomever wanted to come to bring food for a giant potluck, and then to hang out for the afternoon. My mother always provided the meat dish and the drinks. We set up volleyball nets and marked off a flag football field. Eventually we nailed long boards between trees to create permanent serving tables for the meal. The Folk Group became part of the entertainment. On New Year's Day we had a special gathering to listen to the college bowl games. We all gathered around the radios and listened late into the night as the games moved west across America, each bowl finding someone in our group who had something at stake in the outcome. We marked time by Play Days. From the schools, Play Days, and my parents' approach to life, I learned it mattered to surround myself with people who were not like me. The folks that sat around our dinner table were not limited to others from our mission, or other Americans.

When we left Nairobi in 1971, we thought we were coming back. It was time to go on furlough. We put our stuff in storage, sublet the house, and moved back to Fort Worth, which had become a home of its own, in a way, largely because of University Baptist Church and my father's friendship with James Harris, the senior pastor. We had it all planned out: I would go to Paschal High School for my sophomore year and then return to graduate at Nairobi International School alongside of my Folk Group friends. That never happened. Halfway through the year in Texas, my parents decided to accept a one-year assignment from the mission board in Accra, Ghana, which meant I would add another school to my resume, but I would still graduate from NIS. Halfway through the year in Accra my parents decided to resign from the mission board and move back to the States for good. I did not get to go back to Kenya until I was in my forties.

The ending to the chapter of my life that was Nairobi was never clearly written.

A number of years ago a woman named Martha, a classmate at NIS, contacted as many of us as she could and compelled us to get together for a reunion. In a pre–social media world, her undertaking was not easy. We were scattered across the world. The invitation was too good to turn down: I had not seen most of the people in close to thirty years. The school was made up of students whose parents moved around the world for any number of reasons. Many of us were only there for a year or two. All of us spent most of our childhood and adolescence outside of America, moving around. Her invitation was for us to gather at the Chisos Mountain Lodge in the middle of Big Bend National Park, in the southwest corner of Texas. Ginger and I flew from Boston to El Paso and then drove the four hours to the hotel hidden in a valley in the middle of nowhere. As we passed a sign on the interstate that said, "Next exit sixty-five miles," Ginger and I spoke simultaneously.

"This is beautiful," I said.

"There is nothing out here," she said.

Both statements were true. By the time we got to the lodge, most of the others had arrived. We walked into a room of twenty-five or thirty folks who were talking and hugging and laughing. When we got to our room that night, Ginger reflected on what she saw. "The healing was visible," she said. "You could see it on all the faces—as though it was the first time in a long, long time that you were in a room where you were understood, where everyone understood what you had gone through, where you felt normal."

She was right. I had not known that feeling since my family had moved to Houston the middle of my junior year. For the next three or four days we ate and drank and talked and played guitars, singing ourselves deep into the night. Bill Holm writes of reunions and says,

> This moment in most lives gives birth to the longing for connectedness. Partly this longing acknowledges that we cannot escape being tangled into the tissue of history—the long thread of conscious life on the planet. Reunions awaken our curiosity to see how others age, what the world has done to them—for them—in a half century.[11]

On our last evening we drove to the Starlight Lounge in Terlingua, Texas, for a final dinner. We took our instruments with us, much like we did when we all showed up for Play Day. The bartender gave us permission to take the stage (well, take over the stage) and we took turns singing most every song we knew. The whole place sang along. When it was over, the bartender asked if we could come back the next week. We had to tell him no. By then we would be scattered far and wide once more in all the places we had learned to call home.

---

11 Holm, *Heart Can Be Filled*, 190.

CHAPTER 5

Cordone Street

saints of diminished capacity

I only saw the words written,
requiring me to infer tone;
to assume either compassion
or conceit; to decide if the poet
mimed quotation marks when
he said, "diminished capacity,"—
or saints, for that matter—
if he even said the words out loud.

Either way, the phrase is
fragrant with failure, infused
with what might have been,
what came and went,
what once was lost . . .
and now is found faltering,
struggling, stumbling,
still hoping, as saints do,
failure is not the final word.

Forgiveness flows best from
brokenness; the capacity for
love is not diminished by
backs bowed by pain, or
hearts heavy with grief.
Write this down: the substance
of things hoped for fuels
those who walk wounded:
we are not lost; we are loved

I DON'T REMEMBER a time that I did not know of God and Jesus. Christianity was faith, family history, and cultural norm all rolled into one. As a five-year-old, I turned from a life of sin and gave my heart to Jesus, which seemed easy and natural. I could probably count the Sundays we were not in church on one hand. I grew up knowing my parents shared their faith for a job, that bringing people to Jesus was what mattered most. But it was not until we moved to Fort Worth, Texas, and the borrowed brick house on Cordone Street that I confirmed my faith, if you will. What had been handed to me became my own.

If Mwitu was where I learned home was in the middle of a wider world, Cordone Street taught me about a family of faith. Though I had grown up around missionary kids, we were a group because our parents were professional Christians. I loved being at Matero, but the year at University Baptist Church in Fort Worth was the first time I was a part of a youth group, and it was filled with kids who came to church to come to church, to be together. The move from Nairobi to Fort Worth during the summer between my ninth and tenth grade years was expected. That we were moving again had long since ceased to be news and we left expecting to return to Mwitu after my parents' year of furlough. On previous leaves, we had lived in missionary housing; this time we learned of a seminary professor who was going on sabbatical and wanted to rent, which meant we would not have to be in an apartment, but could live in a house in a real American neighborhood: 3362 Cordone Street. The couple who lived there walked out and left the house furnished, so we walked in and sat in their chairs and slept in their beds, as if one play had finished its run and the next began using the same set and props but with different actors.

The small brick house had been built in the fifties as Fort Worth began to grow, but was still close enough to feed into Paschal High and not one of the new suburban schools. I went from a class of fifteen or twenty at NIS to a school with over a thousand students, from a place where we sat on the grass in the middle of a coffee plantation and played guitars to one with all the teams and trappings of American teenage life. Before school started, however, we found our way back to University Baptist Church, which had been our church family on our previous two furloughs and the main reason we chose to live in Fort Worth, and I found myself in the middle of a vibrant American church youth group, which was something I did not even know existed until I was enveloped in love, energy, and acceptance. I have come to understand my tenth grade year as the one where I confirmed my faith, where I understood what it meant for me to follow Christ, or, should I say, I began to understand. My definition is still under construction.

Life in an American high school was unlike anything I had ever experienced. There were more people in my homeroom than in my entire grade in Nairobi, more in my grade than in my entire previous school. My lab partner in biology wore white eye shadow (to match her skin and hair); the girl next to me in English said she was a witch and wore the coolest black cape to class every day. I went to my first pep rally and learned the power of sports in American life. Then there were the things to do— lots of them, and particularly at church. The youth choir practiced twice a week and sang in the early service every Sunday morning. The youth group gathered every Wednesday night and then had all kinds of activities. I was surrounded by all these kids singing and smiling and talking about faith, and including me in the discussion. The person who most befriended me that year was a guy named Mark who played basketball for Paschal and whose family was very active with the youth group. Mark was about six foot eight or ten; I was about five foot two; we were a comedy routine walking down the hall together. He called me "Morty." Being with him and the others in the youth group gave me the first taste of what a true community of faith felt like. It was the early seventies, so we learned and sang the choruses that were coming out of the Jesus Movement and wore big driftwood crosses around our necks. More than that, we looked for each other in the halls of the high school and saved places at the lunch tables. I felt like I belonged.

My bedroom in the house on Cordone Street was small, with enough room for the double bed and a dresser that faced it. A mirror ran across the back of the dresser, so I could sit on the foot of the bed and see myself. In the middle of the swirl of support I found in my youth group, I can also remember sitting there and wishing I could be anyone else. I didn't care who it was; I just didn't want to be me. I don't remember any great crisis, or anything being particularly wrong. I remember I felt short for my age and I felt heavier than I actually was. I had some sense that I was behind in my social development compared to my new American friends, though I could not have articulated it. I lived with the sense of impending doom that if people really knew me they wouldn't want me around. In 1971 none of us knew how to talk about depression, much less recognize it. When I look back now, with what I know about myself, I see the beginnings of the shadows in that room.

The overarching self-image of my adolescence that lives in my memory is that I was a short, fat kid. Over the years I have often viewed my battle of the bulge as a lifelong war because I've always felt chubby, even though, when I look at old pictures, I can see I was not. I grew six inches taller in college, but I never got over feeling heavy. Steve Cloud was the youth minister at the church, and he was everything I was not: athletic, tall, handsome, together. I wanted to be Steve Cloud.

Baptists have two church days each week: Sundays and Wednesdays. At UBC, Wednesday night meant a youth group gathering. In our one-car household, it made more sense for me to walk from Paschal to the church after school and hang out until the evening's festivities began than it did for my parents to figure out how to get me from school to home to church. So after school I would walk down to the Youth House, which was across the street from the church. Steve's office was also there, so I hung out in his office. He called me "Flash." One afternoon, he suggested we go out and shoot some baskets on the church parking lot. I am among the world's worst basketball players, but I went with him. One of my lame two-handed set shots missed everything and the ball rolled across the parking lot.

"You get it," I said disgustedly.

I can still see him walking across, picking up the ball, and walking back toward me with the ball on his hip. He put his arm around me and we turned to go back to his office.

"Flash," he said, "one day Trish and I are going to have a kid and I hope he turns out exactly like you."

That day, Steve gave me a way to imagine myself that helped me live through high school. I wonder sometimes what might have happened if Steve had not said that to me. But he did. In that brief moment on the parking lot, the truth of "yes" found a foothold and hung on for my dear life, giving me a chance to grow into a different image of grace, love, and hope.

I lost track of Steve many years ago. I imagine, however, that if I found him and told him that story and how it changed me, it would not be one he remembered. He was not altering his life that afternoon. He was being himself. He was doing his job. He was living life as he lived it. His passing words gave me the chance to see things differently.

One of childhood images I find hardest to shake is that love is earned. Feeling worthy of love has never come easily for me. As I have said, one of my deepest fears is that I don't belong. In both my head and heart, I can hear the voices of those who love me deeply. I know I am loved and yet I also still hear that it's all conditional because I haven't done enough.

I understand "born again" as a euphemism for conversion, but I don't think it is a one-time thing. What I have learned from my experience and listening to the experiences of others is that we must be born again and again and again if we want to follow Christ. You may remember the story of Jesus and Nicodemus, who came in the dark of night to see Jesus (John 3:1–21). In telling Nicodemus that he must be born again, Jesus was encouraging him to throw out the most basic paradigm of what it meant to be human and allow God to redefine existence. That's not a single act; it has to happen over and over again. Later, using death instead of life as a metaphor, Jesus said it this way: "Take up your cross daily." We read those words and think about Jesus's crucifixion as a model: be willing to sacrifice like he did (not that we really plan to do it)—and we know that his resurrection followed. They heard those words and thought about the way in which criminals were brutally executed: Jesus was calling them to lose everything. Whether talking about life or death, Jesus was deconstructing the very foundations of our existence and reframing what it means to be fully human as he was: born again.

My wife, Ginger, keeps saying she wants me to write a book about how a progressive Christian can have heart faith. Here's where I'll start: I'm a part of the United Church of Christ because I'm born again. I'm not the same guy who gave his heart to Jesus when he was five. Since that time, I've been born again and again and again, leading me to a place in my faith far away from what I learned growing up. What I took with me was a love for good hymn singing, a belief in the power of God to change lives, a heart for service, and gratitude for the way I was taught to study the Bible. Along the way, I was born again when I saw that Paul wasn't kidding when he said in Christ there is no male or female. I was born again when I married Ginger. I was born again when I saw that what is true for gender is also true for sexual orientation. I was born again when I realized that responding to violence with violence accomplishes nothing. I was born again when I sat at the wedding of my good friends Ken and George in Old South Congregational Church. I was born again as I learned how to choose reconciling with my family over my pride and hurt. I am a man of many births. Now God is laboring to give birth to me once more as I seek to find my calling vocationally. All along the way, I have been blessed with an amazing group of midwives who have helped to bring me into these new worlds and even as I struggle to learn to speak and walk anew, I hear Jesus saying, "You must be born again."

Whatever that means for the days to come, I trust Jesus never meant it to be used as a defining label or a condition of membership. I think he did mean to say that none of us has a corner on the truth. It's not about being right; it's about being loved.

CHAPTER 6

Dumfries Street

empty chair

what is
the difference
between
open space
and emptiness?
vacancy
and opportunity?
barrenness
and belief?

in one of
my favorite stories,
a boy named Ian
found a chair
in the shape
of a hand
an open hand
a tender hand
God's hand
to hold him

I drive by
furniture stores
yard sales
sometimes
hoping to see
any chair
that might
offer me the
same invitation

R EADING THE GOSPELS is sometimes like reading e-mail—tone is often hard to convey. Take Mark 3:31–35, for instance:

> Then his mother and his brothers came; and standing outside, they sent to him and called him. A crowd was sitting around him; and they said to him, "Your mother and your brothers and sisters are outside, asking for you."
>
> And he replied, "Who are my mother and my brothers?" And looking at those who sat around him, he said, "Here are my mother and my brothers! Whoever does the will of God is my brother and sister and mother."

How did Jesus sound when he asked who his family was? It's not an easy answer because it doesn't feel much like a Hallmark moment. The tone we infuse into the words makes a difference in how we interpret them. If the words stay in the two-dimensional world of the page, then tone stays out of reach because it needs the three-dimensional world of performance to have room to move. In a time before books, that is how the stories were told. If we want to get to the heart of the stories, then we have to let them live off of the page; we have to incarnate them, we have to perform them. The dictionary says the word "perform" comes from old words that mean to alter and to accomplish. When we tell the story—when we perform it—we alter it by breathing life into it again and we accomplish the task of letting it come alive in us.

One of my favorite liturgists at church is a person named Suzanne. When she reads Scripture, she does it from memory. She tells us the story. She is a part of the Network of Biblical Storytellers, who describe themselves by saying, "We bring God's stories to life for a post-literate, digital age." They are on to something: the gospel story is a living, breathing thing, not something static trapped between book covers. These are stories to be read (aloud) and wrestled with, talked about and talked through, performed and remembered.

Home is where you leave and who you leave. I left home from 5835 Dumfries in the Westbury neighborhood of southwest Houston to go to college. Before this leaving, my family had always left together. Other than my father's business trips, this was the first time any of us had set out on our own and left the rest behind. Leaving Houston was the first time I left by myself and the first time I was told I was leaving home. The rest of my family was staying to grow roots and I was going away.

My parents intended to spend their lives in Africa, so they talked about my brother and me returning to the States for college on our own almost from the time we started school. Each time we came back to America on furlough they drove us to Waco and talked about coming to Baylor, where everyone who had gone to college in our family had gone to college, and how we would find our way halfway around the world from what we knew best. For many missionary kids (MKs), this is the big rite of passage: that time when you try to turn the Far Country into somewhere you actually live rather than visit. I suspect most MKs think they won't stay in America; they are foreign students who have come to get an education. On an institutional level,

Baylor was a sort of home to my family. Everyone who had gone to college went to Jerusalem-on-the-Brazos, including both of my namesakes.

When we arrived in Houston in January of my junior year in high school, my parents were already talking about when I would leave for Waco. From the start, Houston was a way station for me. It was also my most difficult move. When we moved to Houston from Fort Worth, my father's call as pastor of Westbury Baptist Church was not completely certain, which meant we couldn't tell anyone why we were new in town. The new semester was starting, however, and my brother and I needed to be in class. The way the grades were divided, we went to separate schools and both went without knowing anyone. Joining the cast of an American high school halfway through my junior year was like trying to audition for a musical in the middle of the second act: The roles had already been assigned. The worst part of the day was lunch because I was left to a table by myself. Looking back, I think the reason my blog is called *Don't Eat Alone* grew from a seed planted in one of those lonely lunches. I do not like to eat by myself.

As I recollect, it felt as though I went a couple of weeks without anyone talking to me. It may have been a couple of days. What I do remember is the day I heard a voice behind me say, "There he is!" Somehow I knew he was talking about me. A chill went up my spine. I thought perhaps one of the football players had realized I was by myself and was about to make me an unfortunate mascot. Instead it turned out to be a guy named Gordon whose parents were also missionaries in Africa and whom I had known as a little kid in Rhodesia. His family was on leave in Houston and staying in a missionary house provided by the Baptist church closest to the one my father was about to pastor. He had heard through missionary channels that I was there and took it upon himself to find me. He picked up my tray and took me to the table where the youth group from his church ate together. In an instant I was not eating alone. His act of kindness gave me room to find myself in my new surroundings. I joined the choir, made friends, and prepared to go to college.

Leaving home was a big deal to my dad. When I went to college, I was making a break as he had done. I was on my own. My parents redecorated my bedroom and I stayed in the "guest room" for the summers after my freshman and sophomore years. After that second summer I rarely stayed longer than three nights. I had aimed my life in other directions, as I had been taught to do. Even though I was only a few hours down the highway, I was supposed to be a long way off. They were not pushing me away. My parents worked hard to pay for my school and did their best to encourage and support me. My father started Baylor the summer before he turned seventeen because he had nowhere else to go and he wanted an education. For him, college meant setting out on your own, so he offered me the same script.

For my dad, going to Baylor was growing up. When my parents dropped me off for the fall semester, he said, "You will not invest in college life if you come home every weekend. We will see you at Thanksgiving." They came up for some of the football games, but I didn't leave Waco until I got on the Greyhound bus to go to Houston for the holiday. Home became a place to visit.

As the eldest son in our family, I played out the parabolic role in many ways, particularly in my compliance. I did what I was supposed to do. I applied only to Baylor. I was not American enough to know I needed to do a mass mailing of college applications. The family wanted me to go there, so I did. I chose to go into ministry, and particularly to preach, which was the family business. My younger brother did neither. He decided to become a minister of music and moved to the far country of Oklahoma.

One of my fascinations with the parable of the prodigal son is in the father-son dynamics: who leaves, who stays, who waits, who cares, who forgives, who does not, how they continue to try and find each other, and how they learn that leaving does not necessarily mean disconnecting.

Once again, the tone of what is being said in the story is difficult to infer. Most of Jesus's parables are sparse in their details. In almost every case a certain man had two sons, but little else is ever said about them. We get little in the way of description or character development. When the parable of the prodigal son opens, all we see is a kid on the way out the door. We don't know how old he is, what he looks like, or why he wants to leave. We know nothing of their history, nothing of the dynamics between them, and nothing of the sons' mother. As we have told the story over and over, we have filled in details in our interpretation. We could write a volume of short stories about the family based on how we filled in the details. What if the young man left after his mother died and his desire to flee was fueled by his grief? We are never told how long he was gone. Was it a weekend bender, or did he stay away for years? I have often thought Robert Frost's "The Death of the Hired Man" could be read as the prodigal's return as an old man. He came home, only to find nowhere to be.

Home, at least in part, is about family dynamics, about family systems, about what you can count on and what you have to let go. Perhaps the son returned less because he was sure of his father's forgiveness and more because he thought he could still play the old man and appeal to his practical side: let me be a servant. He was not as contrite as he was hungry. However long he was gone, by the time he came back no one was the same. The son had seen too much in the far country, both good and bad, to be the same person who had stormed out in anger, arrogance, or whatever sent him on his way. Who knows what he had done with his bitterness. The older brother seems to have hardened in the meantime, his compliance festering into a simmering fury of envy and entitlement. Since many use the father as the metaphor for God in the story, it's harder to imagine him growing and changing, but something was different. Whatever in the dad had caused the son to leave had tempered into compassion.

The story is distilled to the final scene in many sermons. Henri Nouwen spent a whole book on Rembrandt's painting of the reunion, but there is more to it, just as there's more to home than the nostalgia of what was lost, what was left behind, or what never was. Some places are easier to be from. There is a bit of the prodigal's return in almost all of our comings and goings. A happy meaningful life does not necessarily offer or require a reunion scene; it does, however, require forgiveness if we are to feel at home anywhere. If I am not going back, I have to find a way to let go, to remember with kindness and hope.

Much like Paul's admonition to make things right before coming to the Communion table, any coming home means asking what needs to be made right, who needs to be forgiven, from whom forgiveness needs to be asked, and what has not been said that needs to be voiced, and then to ask, "When do we eat?"

Home, in this story, is closely tied to family of origin, or at least to the people who raised us and grew up alongside of us. One of the hazards of familiarity is that we can easily let things go unspoken—we learn to live with them, we say. Those small silent stones stack up into walls if we don't keep the channels clear and current in our goings out and comings in.

I have tried to picture the days after the son's return and the years that followed. As an older sibling, I come back to wondering what conversations took place between the brothers. How did they work it out? Did the elder one ever get over his anger? Did he stay once his kid brother was back? As John Denver used to sing, we've got new names and faces, but the gospel changes are still going down.

In all our years of education, my brother and I ended up in the same school only a couple of times. The high school in Houston served only grades ten though twelve, so Miller and I were in high school together only during my senior year. He and I both loved to sing. He was beginning to feel called into vocational music ministry. Music was becoming more and more important to him, yet he didn't join the choir at school because I was already in it. The same was true of drama class and student council. Only after I graduated did he come into his own. He was the lead in the spring musical his last two years and student council president as a senior. He then chose to go to college somewhere other than where I was.

We have never really talked about those days or those choices. I am speaking from my vantage point as his older brother. I didn't feel slighted as much as separated. He and I have never really figured out how to be essential to one another. We had enough on our own plates in high school and college to keep me from wondering too much about the other; we were not in the same place, and we were young. Then I read the parable and I'm pulled to ponder the space between us.

My parents lived in the house on Dumfries for fifteen years after I left to go to college. It was their home to which I returned from college, from seminary. I came back there from Fort Worth and Dallas. Ginger and I had moved to Boston before Dad retired and they moved to Waco. Though I never felt like Houston was my hometown, my parents' home was there, which meant it was my home in some sense, though the house was disconnected from most of my history. Houston was not a place I wanted to go back to very much, but it was where my parents lived. It was another home I left.

My connection to the prodigal parable is through my recurring question of how parents and children let each other grow up and come in and out of each other's lives. What are the patterns and rituals we set, the way we say hello and good-bye, and the way we stay connected? Much of our adult life concerns how we come and go from one another. Home is the place you leave, and to which you return and then leave again. Cue the psalmist once more: God bless us in our going out and in our coming home.

CHAPTER 7

Walraven Avenue

best of friends

hide and seek snakes and ladders
I remember when
you and me and all that matters
best of times best of friends

these days of sunshine these days of rain
we pull together in days of pain
we share beginnings we share the ends
itha worth it all in these days to be best of friends

stand and fall hurt and healing
say goodbye again
through it all the gift of feeling
worst of times still best of friends

these days of sunshine these days of rain
we pull together in days of pain
we share beginnings we share the ends
itha worth it all in these days to be best of friends

here and now make a promise
and take it to the end
heart to heart God is in us
all the time the best of friends

these days of sunshine these days of rain
we pull together in days of pain
we share beginnings we share the ends
itha worth it all in these days to be best of friends[12]

---

12 Crockett/Brasher-Cunningham, *The Basic Stuff*, Walking Angel Records. ©1990 Spare Room Music. Used by permission.

THE LIFE I PICTURED after seminary was in Switzerland. As my college and seminary friends were signing up to stay in Fort Worth for doctoral work, or preparing to pastor in Texas, one of my professors who had studied at the University of Basel encouraged me to apply. He helped me write letters and begin to plan, which is when I discovered I would have to wait a year to start the program. I applied for a Clinical Pastoral Education Internship (CPE) at Baylor University Medical Center in Dallas and was accepted. The chance to study in Switzerland never materialized and the year at Baylor grew into a second internship and then a staff position; I stayed there almost four years. During those days, I began to lead youth retreats. In the summer of 1984, a man named James Carter, pastor of University Baptist Church in Fort Worth, called and said, "A little bird told me you might be interested in being a youth minister." By that fall, I was sitting in the office where Steve Cloud had called me "Flash."

To be a youth minister in the 80s was to live in the Golden Age: U2, REM, and the Indigo Girls were all getting started, John Hughes was making movies about teenage life, Mr. Miagi was teaching the Karate Kid how to rise up, and Robin Williams was Mr. Keating. Minister to Youth at University Baptist Church in Fort Worth was my first job not related to school. I had worked as a hospital chaplain at Baylor Medical Center, but I had moved into that position from a two-year CPE residency. I spent my weekends on youth retreats and my vacation at youth camp in the summer, thanks to my friends who were youth ministers around the state. When the chance came, I stepped into my first real adult gig: hanging out with kids.

University Baptist was the church my family had attended when we were on furlough from Africa. It was where I learned what a youth group was. Now it was my job to help build one. So many of the people who made up the core of our group had grown up together in school and at church, had lived in the same houses, and had known a life I did not. Like Ezra in Anne Tyler's novel *Dinner at the Homesick Restaurant,* I was trying to create a sense of belonging I had only brushed up against, only tasted. The kids already knew how to do it. They taught me how to belong and, for the first time in my life, I had a chance to be the one who stayed. When graduation came each spring we sent the seniors on their way and I stayed behind. I had to live with their absence. I had never done that before. Home, I learned, was where people leave you behind.

When I first moved to town, I found a small run-down house, but then a woman in the church had to move into assisted living and wanted to rent rather than sell, so I moved to Walraven Street and a 1960s tract house, which meant it didn't have much character, but it had three bedrooms and a big backyard. Before long I had a dog—Bear, a big black lab–golden mix—who was a big ball of love. He jumped the fence every day after I left for work to walk with the group of women who circled our neighborhood, or so I found out about a year later when I met them while out walking with him one afternoon. The decor in the house was stereotypical early single male and was made up mostly of stuff other people no longer wanted, the highlight of which was a seven-foot-long, three-legged green couch (propped up with old books) that was home to an incredibly vigilant nap monster. I also shared the space and the rent with Dale, a seminarian and church member who had both a dog and a room of his own. The house on Walraven was the right place at the right time.

My approach to youth ministry was deeply influenced by Gene Wilkes, a seminary friend who was a youth minister in Richardson, Texas. He invited me to come to youth camp the summer before James Carter called me, and the week with his youth group opened my heart to youth ministry. I had never seen youth camp done with such imagination. The point of the week was to make sure everyone knew they were loved and they belonged.

The musician for camp was Billy Crockett. Our friendship started as we sat up late and looked down over the river at Camp Ozark. When I took the job at University Baptist Church we began writing songs, or, I should say, I began writing lyrics to fit his melodies and he sang and recorded them. Those songs grew out of our friendship and my life with the youth group. The first one was called "Here's Another Picture,"[13] which we wrote for my first camp with UBC. The chorus says:

> here's another picture of life
> all of us together with Christ
> it's an open heart
> it's a work of art
> it's the basic stuff
> that makes another picture of love

UBC was where I learned my most important lessons about teaching, even before I saw myself as a teacher. Early in my time

---

13 Crockett/Brasher-Cunningham, *The Basic Stuff*, Walking Angel Records. ©1990 Radar Days Music. Used by permission.

there, I was facilitating a Sunday school teacher training and asked Jeter Basden to lead the session. Jeter was a professor at the seminary in Fort Worth and, along with his wife, Claudette, directed our college Sunday school class. He began by writing one sentence on the blackboard we had rolled into the fellowship hall:

I teach students the Bible.

He stepped back and said, "Tell me the direct object of the verb and I will tell you what kind of teacher you are going to be." After some discussion, he concluded, "If you think you teach the Bible, you will quickly lose contact with the kids; if you think you teach students, you can read from the phone book and change their lives." His observation remains tattooed into my consciousness. He gave words to what I have found true whether at church, in a kitchen, or in a classroom: teaching is a fundamentally relational act.

What I learned at UBC was that the point of life or ministry wasn't to make the kids into something as much as it was to be with them, and to help them to learn more about how to be together. In many ways, they knew more about creating community than I did. Many of them had not only been around their extended family their whole lives, they had lived next door to the same people, they had gone to school together; they had a whole city they knew by heart. They knew how to stay far better than I. Together we built rituals and traditions, spoke in movie lines and song lyrics, learned that questions were better than answers, and gave ourselves permission to relax and enjoy the ride. We were intentional about figuring out every way we could to let each other know we were loved—by God, by each other. Loved. Period. Loved, loved, loved. Home is where you belong.

I had been in Fort Worth about three years when I realized I didn't know how to stay. I began going to therapy to get some help in learning how to grow roots. I did not want to go any-where and I was afraid I would set myself up to leave by default. Several weeks into our meetings, my doctor said, "Somewhere along the way when you were very young—probably before you were five—you learned love was earned."

I began to talk about how much my parents always said they loved me and were proud of me and he made an important dis-tinction between what I was taught and what I learned. The two, he pointed out, are not always the same. My task, as an adult, was to unlearn the lessons, reteach myself, and rewrite the script.

I remember waking up one morning about six months into therapy and feeling differently about myself. I felt like I was worth something. I liked me. In the same town where I had sat on the edge of the bed as a tenth grader and wished to be someone else, I felt content to be me. When I told my therapist what had hap-pened, his eyes welled up and he said, "That's the best news I've heard in a while." Then he said, "No one can take this away from you. Remember that. You don't lose this ground."

As much as I loved being somewhere I wanted to stay, I thought part of my calling was to launch our young people out into the world. Staying forever was not the obvious choice to me. After all, Jesus said, "Go into all the world. . . ." The first mission trip I planned was to inner city Chicago, replacing the annual ski trip. One of the parents came to tell me he was not going to let his daughter go because he didn't think it was safe. She had been skiing, but somehow working in an urban church food pantry felt more dangerous than flying down a black diamond. I pressed him a bit and he said, "I'm afraid if she goes there she won't want to stay here."

"I hope so," I answered, as though I knew moving was better than staying. Those whose worlds I sought to expand taught me how to stay and I did—for six years. One of the things Ginger often reminds our congregation of is that we are called in Christ to choose relationships over doctrine. Somehow I knew that to be true when I was in Fort Worth, though I didn't know how to articulate it in quite that way. The people who were in that youth group run the spectrum theologically as adults, and as many of them are still in Fort Worth as are scattered across the country and the world. The line from Walt Whitman, via Robin Williams, is one we repeated over and over: "The powerful play goes on and you can contribute a verse."

The verse I had to contribute changed in January 1989 when I met Ginger on a winter youth retreat for a group of Texas churches. She was a sponsor with the church I had attended in Dallas during my chaplaincy days and she was a chaplain intern at Baylor Medical Center. Since it turned out so well, I can say I followed her around all weekend until she agreed to go out with me. We were engaged in August of that year and married in April 1990, which opened my eyes to the best definition of home I had ever known: being with her.

CHAPTER 8

Hill Street

snap shot

what I remember may not be how it
happened; every time I go back to a
memory the light in the room is a bit
different, or people have changed clothes.

I recall standing under the light post
wrapped up in Christmas garland—the light post,
that is—you in your big purple coat
and I with long dark hair, even on top.

We made the front page of the *Patriot*.
It was a long time ago. Yet, once my
memory begins to animate the scene,
and we are side by side on the streets

of Charlestown: cobblestone and chilly winds,
my heart is exposed once more to all the
years of open invitations in your eyes
I have answered since that one Sunday.

We stood there in the cold long enough
for the camera to catch and release us
to all the other afternoons where we
have walked—even when no one had a camera

GINGER AND I MARRIED in April of 1990 and moved to Boston in August. Neither of us had ever lived there or had family there or had any reason to go there other than it felt like it was the right thing to do. We felt called. The previous December we heard a woman named Betsey Draper speak at a missions conference in Fort Worth. She was a chaplain at MIT. Ginger leaned over to me and said, "One day, we will live in Boston and we will be friends with her." The following Monday, the senior pastor at University Baptist Church, where I was youth minister, called me in to his office to share a dream about our congregation helping to start new churches in other cities. He looked across the desk with confidence and said, "I think the first one should be in Boston and I think Ginger and you should be the ones to plant it." He knew nothing of our Saturday night experience. As I said, we felt called. The way things had rolled out made us all believe there was something in it worth chasing down. By Labor Day we had packed our belongings into a big Hertz-Penske truck and driven ourselves and our Schnauzer, Reuben, to our new adventure. And, yes, we did become friends with Betsey.

To say things did not turn out as we expected would not be accurate because we had no idea what to expect. We had never lived in Boston. We had never started a church. We had never gotten married and moved across the country. Yet there we were, together in Boston, trying to figure it all out. When I lived in Dallas I saw a one-act play called "The Actor's Nightmare." The premise of the play was the actor woke up to find himself on stage in the middle of a show. He was in costume and the stage was filled with other actors. The problem was he had no idea what play was being performed or what character he was portraying. The other actors delivered their lines and waited for his response and the best he could do was improvise. Just when he figured out he was in Noel Coward's *Private Lives*, the play changed to something else.

Though Boston was by no means a nightmare, our lives resonated with the play. The way University Baptist Church had chosen to finance the endeavor meant both Ginger and I had to find other jobs alongside our experiment in evangelism. We both started in retail, then she became the youth minister at First Congregational, Winchester UCC and I signed up to be a substitute teacher in the Boston public schools, both of which became full-time gigs. We had a weekly Bible study that met in our little second-floor apartment. As each day passed, we felt more and more as though we were choosing Boston as our hometown and it was choosing us.

The early nineties were the end of a downward cycle in real-estate prices in New England. We decided we wanted to buy a house before things heated up again. With the help of a realtor we had gotten to know, we began looking at property in our neighborhood and, after several failed attempts, managed to buy 14 Hill Street, a small row house on a one-way, dead-end street. It was our third address as a married couple and our first house. We moved our stuff, our Schnauzers, and our fledgling Bible study up over the top of Bunker Hill to our new place: our new home.

The house on Hill Street was the first place we owned, the first place without a lease, the first place where we planned to stay together. It was the house on the end of a line of five row houses. As best we could tell from our research at the Registry of Deeds, it was built sometime in the 1840s. The house went straight up and down: fourteen hundred square feet on four floors, including a basement that had an alley entrance because of the steep slope of Bunker Hill as it rolled down into the Mystic River. Each floor had two rooms and a staircase, topped off by a room where the attic had been that became our bedroom once we added a closet. The place was unique in our neighborhood because it had a side yard, created decades earlier when the house that had stood in that space burned down. The person who owned our place at the time bought the lot for $126 in unpaid taxes.

The house needed work. Though some renovations had been done through the years, much of it was as it had been from the start, save a layer of wallboard or a coat of paint. We took on the task of renovating our home. "Renovate" means "to renew" in its original Latin form. What we hoped for our house was to give it a fresh start, to breathe new life into the old bones. We tore out the walls original to the house and put up sheetrock. I wondered what stories escaped in the air that had been trapped for one hundred and fifty years. I saved the old square head nails that held the boards in place. We collected the small bottles and trinkets we found in the walls. We poured a concrete floor over the dirt one in the basement and I learned to lay ceramic tile and wished I had had a chance to practice the skill before it mattered. As we renovated the house we redid the side yard as well. We built a fence and then lined it with planters and pots, planted a Rose of Sharon tree, and even laid a stone patio. I made enough trips to Home Depot that the cashier thanked me for putting his kid through college.

My favorite part of the renovation was the kitchen. For the first time, we were able to build a room based on what we hoped would happen there. The room was small, square, and poorly designed. To move between sink and stove and fridge meant

crossing the room and bumping into someone. We took everything down to the wall studs and floor joists so we could make
it all as large and level as possible and that meant tearing out
the old plaster and lathe, which was how they made walls before
there was sheetrock. Inch-wide furring strips were nailed across
the wooden studs and then plaster was, well, plastered over them
to create a smooth and solid wall. For a couple of weeks during
construction we could stand on the floor joists in the kitchen
and see into the basement. We could, but our Schnauzers could
not. Since the way to the side yard was through the kitchen, we
had to channel our inner gymnasts and balance on the beams as
we passed the Schnauzers like a bucket brigade so they could go
outside.

The kitchen was the entrance to our home; we wanted it to
be an invitation. Once someone came through the front door
and the small entry, they were in the kitchen. The front windows ran along one wall; on the opposite side was a half wall and
counter that opened into the dining room. The entire first floor
was about cooking and eating together. I placed the stove, sink,
fridge, and island in such a way that I could do what I needed
to do to cook while the room was full of people and not have to
ask anyone to get out of the way. I wanted them to stay. That was
the point.

As the house changed, so did our lives in Boston. We had
both found full-time jobs that we loved even as our Bible study
group faded away, thanks to a winter of twelve blizzards, all of
which seem to fall on Bible study night. By the time spring came,
snow and circumstance had scattered our little band. Some had
moved, some had found other congregations; we were back to
Square One. There was no group, no church, just people we saw
periodically. We had failed in our original purpose. Still, we knew
we belonged in Boston, but not for the reasons we first imagined.

As we had renovated the house, we had to renovate our calling. We wrote the church in Fort Worth to tell them of the change in our direction. They responded graciously and wished us well.

Boston is where Ginger and I grew up together, where we learned how to live, as Wendell Berry says, in "the country of marriage."[14] We were born other places, we lived other places, but Boston became our hometown because we let it get inside us. For the first time in our lives we lived in a town where it was easier to walk than to drive and find a parking place. We traversed the city and wore ourselves out day after day. We learned the bus and train schedules, we walked up and down the narrow streets. We stood in line to get tickets to see the Sox play at Fenway, even in the years they didn't win. We learned how to give directions by landmarks like Dunkin' Donuts and Kappy's Liquors since there were very few street signs to reference.

U2 sang about walking where the streets have no name. Boston was the first city where I felt like the streets knew my name, which is another way to define home: I know the streets and the streets know me. I pounded my presence into the pavement after years of walking, riding, and finding my way across the city. When we first moved to the neighborhood of Charlestown, we came home tired each night because we had never walked so much in our lives. When the time came that we had to have a car for our jobs, we had to learn our directions all over again because how we walked somewhere was not how we could drive there. To know a city by foot or by mass transit is different than knowing it by car. Walking a city is learning it in real time, in slower motion, engaging the city on a cellular level: sights, smells, sounds, cracks in the sidewalk. I didn't just drive by the shops, I heard the voices from inside, I smelled the smells. I entered their

14 Wendell Berry, *New Collected Poems* (Berkeley, CA: Counterpoint, 2012), 167.

orbit, even if just for a moment. To walk a city is to be in conversation, in relationship with the place where you live.

Martin Heidegger said:

> The Old English and High German word for building, *buan*, means to dwell. This signifies: to remain, to stay in a place. The real meaning of the verb *bauen*, namely, to dwell, has been lost to us. But a covert trace of it has been preserved in the German word *Nachbar*, neighbor. The neighbor is in Old English the n*eahgehur*; *neah*, near, and *gebur*, dweller.[15]

There is a certain analog quality to living in an East Coast city because the houses are so close and so few have central air conditioning, which means during the summer we share more with one another than perhaps we intended. Life is lived with the windows open. Within weeks we knew what people liked to cook for dinner, what names they called each other when they were angry, and what they watched on television. We might not speak to passing strangers on the sidewalk, but what we did and said at home was live theater for the near-dwellers.

We moved from Texas, which is a place that prides itself on being friendly; you speak to strangers as you pass on the street. In many ways, however, that kind of hospitality doesn't necessarily mean there is a relationship, or that things grow deeper. The downtown neighborhoods of Boston have historically been tight-knit communities, often gathered around an ethnic

15 Martin Heidegger, "Building Dwelling Thinking," in *Poetry, Language, Thought*, trans. Albert Hofstadter (New York: Harper Colophon Books, 1971), http://mysite.pratt.edu/~arch543p/readings/Heidegger.html.

heritage. Charlestown's history was blue collar and Irish. We moved there as the neighborhood, which is one square mile and houses around 16,000 people, was beginning to gentrify. We had to show we were there to do more than make a killing on real estate.

Collier's Grocery was a small market and sandwich shop on Bunker Hill Street that stood between our house on Hill Street and Charlestown High School, where I taught. They made a cheeseburger sub that is still the best I have ever had. No. That anyone has ever had. About once a week I would stop on my way home from school and get a sandwich. After about six months the woman behind the counter asked with a strong Boston accent, "You've come in here long enough. What's your name?" I told her and she replied, "My name's Lynn." When I started to explain where I lived she broke in, "You live on Hill Street, your wife's a ministah, and you teach down the high school. It was just time to learn your name."

From that point on we were at home at Collier's. Ginger's sandwich of choice was the turkey club, which was not an everyday creation. I would call the shop and ask Mr. Collier if it was on the menu and he would answer with a question:

"Is this for that gah-jus wife of yahs?"

"Yes," I would reply.

"Give me twenty minutes. I'll make it if it's for her."

Those who were born and raised on our little urban island of a neighborhood called themselves "Townies." I was not one. I was not trying to be or become one, and still we belonged there. We were at home in our little house on our one-way, dead-end street around the corner from the sub shop.

How does a place get inside you? It's in my blood, we say. In my bones. I think of Boston and the things it holds that I can't find in other places. The push of air that comes like a sideways breeze as the train comes into the T station. The two guys at our neighborhood Dunkin' Donuts who knew the orders of their regulars without speaking. The smell of the heat radiating from the hot water pipes that ran around the baseboards.

At 14 Hill Street, we realized our attempt to start a church had failed, found our way to the United Church of Christ, each earned additional graduate degrees, worked our way into jobs we loved, ate our fair share of cheeseburger subs and turkey clubs, and kept working on the house. Renovating an old home requires that one live in the creative tension between what stays and what goes away. We were not restoring the house the way one might bring a worn work of art back to its former glory to enhance a museum collection. Neither were we reconstructing the place, as one might create a replica of an old ship. They restored the USS Constitution while we lived in Charlestown. Since it was still a commissioned vessel they were allowed to use new materials. Had it been out of commission, they would not have been able to alter a thing. With sailors on board, it was still a work in progress.

Refresh, as in update, renovate, make new again. We had changes we wanted to make, and we still wanted it to be 14 Hill Street. We weren't razing the place to start from scratch. The building had stories written in the wood and walls, in the air that was finally released when the plaster was pulled away. We were adding another chapter.

We did our share of tearing out, particularly the old plaster and lathe, which was how they made walls before there was sheetrock. Inch-wide furring strips were nailed across the wooden studs and then plaster was, well, plastered, over them to create a smooth and solid wall. By the time all of it was removed, along with an unused chimney, we estimated we helped our house lose about two thousand pounds. Until then, I had never thought about how much a house might weigh. We didn't want to retrofit a modern interior over the old bones, even though we planned to add some conveniences and appliances our predecessors would not have recognized. We wanted the house to feel like itself, to be true to its history, and to be refreshed in the telling of its story, which also serves as metaphor for how to build a marriage. A home. When Ginger and I got married we both had some renovating to do, if you will—some changes to make—in order to accommodate all that we let in when we decided to live life together. Marriage, perhaps, doesn't require a complete makeover, but a renovation to accommodate new promises made is certainly in order. We both brought our history and what we had each built to that point and together we renovated our lives into a new relationship.

Life together means reconstructing our points of view from just "me" to include "we." If I use the rent versus own analogy, the freedom of renting is that you can always walk away. The risk is that your landlord can as well. The mortgage makes for higher stakes and deeper roots. Marriage is not about ownership, but it is about committing to stay, which means the stakes are higher. Boston became our hometown because we changed there on purpose. We discovered something there. We learned how to be together there, and we also learned we would leave together, that home would not be just one place. Home means something different when you're not the only one there and when the one with whom you share it wasn't born there. You both chose to stay.

There aren't many marriage stories in Scripture that relate to marriage as we know it now. Adam and Eve just showed up together. We can name Abraham and Sarah, but he slept with a servant when it appeared Sarah could not have children. Jacob loved Rachel, but had to marry Leah as well. We know little about Mary and Joseph from what we read in the Gospels. We have verses we pull out to prove our points, but the real guidelines for relational equality and abiding love are found in verses that offer a larger relational focus that we can bring to bear on what marriage means in our time and in our culture. Ginger and I knew we loved each other and wanted to spend our lives together. We also knew we were not called to have children of our own, which meant, for us, that we would create a home with an open door. In twenty-five years of marriage, we have had seventeen different people live with us.

When it comes to marriage, we learn first from what we see, which is also true of gender roles. What I saw with my parents was that they were kind to one another. They worked hard not to do damage, not to say things in anger they could not take back. I also saw how much they enjoyed being together. They took their promises seriously. Ginger's parents had a strong and loving relationship as well. We had good examples. Like us, our parents liked each other as well as loved each other. We didn't mimic them, but we are grateful we were given models of what love looked like.

What marriage means has evolved over the centuries, as has what it means to be human. We have moved, for example, from "How do I make a fire and not get killed by wild animals?" to "How does social media affect my humanity?" We have those questions that remain at the core ("Why am I here?"), but how we articulate them has evolved. Irenaeus imagined that Adam and Eve were created as children. The temptation of the Tree of Knowledge was the lure of growing up too quickly. Human history is the story of human growth, development, and understanding. We are called to renovate our philosophies and theologies as we understand more about the tenaciously inclusive love of God.

Looking back through history, the earliest understandings of marriage centered primarily on procreation and property: how things were handed down and to whom. In our age of displacement in which so many of us are dislocated and relocated, home is more about who than where, which means how we choose to define what it means to be together. To be married in these days is more about how the love that is created gets lived out, how the promises are kept, and how our love for one another reconnects with the Love that breathed the universe into existence.

I am not saying marriage is the only way that happens. How we treat one another, how we love one another is at the core of what it means to be human. Marriage is one of the living metaphors of home that helps us articulate how we incarnate love. In the same way the promises made in taking each other for richer and poorer and in sickness or health are lived out in daily choices, we have to choose each other over convenience and comfort on both big and small levels, particularly those of us who are the privileged ones. We must work to renovate our world into a home where everyone feels essential. Society, in a way, is under constant renovation and renewal, much like a strong marriage. We have to keep fixing things, improving things, cleaning things to make our home livable and loving.

What marriage means to me is I am choosing to make Ginger essential to my life: to make her my home. When I choose to see marriage as a metaphor of home on a larger scale I am invited to see those around me as essential as well. The places we live are too easily populated by people who remain nameless and invisible to us if we are not intentional about choosing them. Ginger and I talk often about how much life in America seems structured to require a raft of minimum wage workers so that we can feel comfortable. How do we get to know the people at the dry cleaners and the grocery store? How do we choose to make them essential rather than merely necessary? How do we make a place where we all feel at home?

There is a sense in which home is our primary perspective on life, our vantage point: The View from Here. The definition is less place and more point of view—the fundamental us. At home we hold the way we respond to the world around us: fear, hope, disappointment, cynicism, skepticism, faith, trust, love. Herein lies the reason we can look at the same circumstance and see things differently. The eyes of There Is Not Enough will see things differently than those of Everyone Belongs. Those who know of security and comfort will see the world more kindly than those who worry about where they will find their next meal. The eyes of the one behind the counter at the dry cleaners will see things differently than the one picking up shirts and dresses. Our point of view is also affected by what we think home is: something to be protected or something to be shared. Hill Street was where I learned how we renovate our lives to make room for one another. Home is life together.

CHAPTER 9

Bay Street

what the tide takes away

we walk the same stretch
of sand when the tide
is low to see how
the waves that wandered
up to the sea wall
have reshaped the beach
before they ran back.

we pace the packed sand
dropping words among
the rocks and driftwood,
the shells and sea glass,
pounding our feelings
with each step, leaving
them behind like footprints.

we are not walking
away from it all;
we are together,
leaving a trail of
feelings at low tide,
on our way home.

tonight as we sleep
the tide will come in
up to the seawall,
wiping the sand clean
of our footprints . . .
a gesture of forgiveness.

T HE HOUSE WE CALLED home in Marshfield sat six hundred and fifty feet from Cape Cod Bay. When we moved there, I stepped out of ten years as an English teacher so I could write. Back then I was chasing the Great American Novel and had managed to write a draft of one while I was teaching at Charlestown High School, always imagining that I could write more if I just had more time and the rest of life's promises took a step back. After nine years as an associate, Ginger was ready to be a senior pastor, so she began the process of sending out her profile and interviewing with UCC churches in and around Boston. We had pointed our view north of the city, but North Community Church in Marshfield caught us by surprise and we soon found ourselves packing and moving to what Bostonians know as the South Shore, which takes in the towns between Boston and Cape Cod.

To live at the beach means you have to learn the tides. Before I lived by the water, I had no sense that the tides came and went at different times, much less that the highs and lows happened twice a day. We learned to mark time by the tides, and we learned to adapt to them. We had no choice. To stand on our beach and look out was to face due east. Though the waters in front of us were part of Cape Cod Bay, the tip of the Cape that was Provincetown was farther south, so there was no land to see, only ocean. We were at the edge of the continent, the border of our country, the end of the land and the expanse of ocean was a reminder of what we came to call our appropriate insignificance: the reminder that we are wonderfully and uniquely created in the image of God and worthy to be loved and no more so than anyone else. It matters both that we are here and that we are not that big of a deal.

In Green Harbor, our neighborhood, the water came all the way to the sea wall at high tide. The beach completely disappeared. When the tide receded, it left the beach looking different almost every day. The sand might be smooth and clean one day, or there might be a covering of little tiny pebbles flecked with sea glass that made the water sound like applause as it pulled back into the ocean. One day would bring a layer of baseball-sized stones and the next, rocks so big you needed two hands to pick them up.

As we were leaving Charlestown, we marked the months and weeks with losses. Our beloved Schnauzer, Hannah, died of congestive heart failure. She was our Boston mascot in so many ways and knew every person in Charlestown who carried cookies in their pockets and they knew her. My only aunt, Pegi, who had been my lifeline to my family in those years when I didn't know how to stay connected, and Ginger's Aunt Virginia, for whom she was named, both died. The house in Green Harbor was the first one none of them knew about and that didn't know about them. It was also the house where I first learned to name my depression.

The fall I fell into darkness was supposed to be the beginning of My Year to Write. While we were in Charlestown, I had gone to the Humber School for Writers the summer before I turned forty and then continued in a correspondence class working with Timothy Findley to complete a novel. Our move to Marshfield meant I was too far away to drive back and forth across the city to keep teaching in Winchester, so we decided I would take a year off from teaching and see what I could make of it. When September came, what I did, for the most part, was get out of bed, walk up and down the beach picking up bits of sea glass, and write rather morose poetry.

When I tell the story, I talk about how the ground opened up on Labor Day weekend 2001, sending me into an emotional and spiritual free fall. I have been questioned at times by others living with depression whose experience has been that depression shows up all at once. As I look back, I can see what felt like an ambush had been festering for some time. My world had been collapsing in ways I didn't understand and that weekend was when I began to come to terms with what had already been crashing down. In December of 2000, I went to the doctor because it felt as though every time I sat down for more than a few minutes I fell asleep. For most of my life I had existed on anywhere from four to six hours of sleep a night. That did not work anymore. She told me I was sleep deprived and that she thought I had sleep apnea. Once I went through the overnight testing at Sleep Camp, as Ginger and I called it, and they gave me a Snuffleupagus machine (our name for the CPAP), I felt rested for the first time I could remember. The apnea, however, had masked the depression. Once I was no longer sleep deprived, there was room to fall deeper into the darkness.

Looking back further still, my therapist in Fort Worth had looked at my psychological testing and told me I was on the borderline of being clinically depressed, but in 1987 we didn't really know what to do with it. I also look back at the tenth grader sitting on the edge of my bed wishing I were someone else even when nothing seemed wrong, and I wonder if my body chemistry wasn't trying to tell me something. The circumstances are only part of the story. I live with depression whether it's high tide or neap; it is in me. However it began, however it simmered inside, on that weekend in 2001 it showed up to stay. I had to learn to live with it, to live through it, to be at home with it.

A recent story on NPR[16] marked the twenty-fifth anniversary of William Styron's *Darkness Visible*, which was first published in *Vanity Fair*. I read it in book form somewhere around 2002, thanks to another therapist. The reporter talked about the impact the essay had in opening up the public conversation about depression because Styron was so open about his struggle from the midst of it, rather than a here's-what-I-went-through perspective of hindsight. He also talked about depression not necessarily having a circumstantial cause, but being a function of body chemistry, being something with which we learn to live.

As a young adolescent, I remember Thomas Eagleton stepping down as a vice presidential candidate because of published reports that he had been treated for depression. People questioned his fitness for leadership. When I think back on listening to those Voice of America radio reports, or reading them in Dad's *TIME* magazine, I remember feeling profoundly sad, even though I didn't know much about what was going on. My recollection of the scene gives me a sense of resonance. Somehow, perhaps, I knew then I was a member of his tribe.

As I began to learn how to live with depression, I began looking for metaphors, and particularly nonbattle metaphors. I have never been much of a Christian soldier, or a soldier of any kind; going to battle does not help me to sort out what's going on, or give me an explanation that offers options. I resonate with struggle and working hard, but I learned that my depression was a bit like the tides: it kept coming and I could no more fight it than I could stop the waves from covering our beach when the tide came in. I do not mean I gave up, or even that I surrendered. I went in search of more creative and less violent ways to think

---

16 Morning Edition, National Public Radio, "25 Years Ago, 'Darkness Visible' Broke Ground Detailing Depression," December 17, 2014.

about how I might answer or respond to the darkness that enveloped me.

I felt like an elephant was sitting on my shoulders. I felt like I was chasing the pin spot at the end of a silent movie, trying to stay close enough that the light didn't completely disappear. I began to learn ways to connect—reconnect—fragments of light and life to change how I felt.

Part of the depression was learning that what I thought I left behind followed me. In all of our moves we have worked hard to cull what we pack into the moving boxes only to find we still have things to throw away when we unpack at the new place. When the darkness came to light that Labor Day I realized traces of what was weighing me down ran back through most of my life.

For the depression to land in September meant it deepened as the New England days grew shorter heading into winter. On a cloudy day, both the sky and the house would be dark by three or four. If I were in the house as the night fell, I fell right along with it. If I got out of the house, I could come home after dark and survive. On many an afternoon, I would ride along with Ginger to her appointments and sit on the other side of the coffee shop with a book or a journal until she was done and then we would come home to the darkness together. Together. Home became a refuge, a place I could be depressed, and grew to be a place I could live through it.

The Saturday after the free fall began Ginger came to me and said, "I have to ask you to do something difficult." She went on to say she thought I needed to stand up in church during what we call the "prayers of the people" and ask for prayer and say out loud I was depressed. She couldn't do it for me; I needed to do it myself. There is great power in being known. In recollecting the pieces of that moment I can see that even in her grief and distress she knew me, her extroverted husband, and she knew I needed to be reminded that I was not alone.

When the time came in the service, I stood up and said something like, "I am dealing with a deep depression and I have never felt like this before. I need your prayers." At coffee hour three people came up to me privately and said, "I didn't know we could talk about this out loud." Their words gave me a hint of the tenacious tethers that bind us to one another, enabled me to recall what I knew to be true, and helped me to begin to remember me. It was not an easy task. Or, I should say, it is not an easy task. The journey is ongoing and each day I am reminded—shown again—of the necessity of community and the abiding character of connectedness.

I shaved my head in October of 2001, about six weeks after I started coming to terms with my depression. I had had close to shoulder length hair for years, and was already coming to terms with my expanding forehead. A good pair of wire-rimmed glasses and I could have passed for Ben Franklin. Shaving my head allowed me, as I came to say, to make the inevitable look like a choice. I suppose it was also a way to make the depression not feel inevitable or final. I could change me. The choice was mine. I was not trapped in the downward spiral. The youth group was raising money for a service trip the following summer, so I turned my haircut into a fundraiser and asked people to pay to watch me get my head shaved during coffee hour. Tom, one of our parishioners, had a shaved head, so he went to work on mine and a pair of scissors, a pile of locks, a couple of blades, and four hundred dollars in donations later, I was a changed man.

The following spring Ginger had another word of wisdom. I needed to find work, both for my physical health and our financial well-being. I spent a week or two driving around the South Shore towns looking for something I could do. I got one job at a small summer concert venue because it meant I could hear music for free. I went in hoping to be a stage hand; my shaved head got me a security gig.

In my quest for employment, I also found a little place called the Tamarind Tea House that was preparing to open. It had about thirty seats and was owned by a woman who had always wanted to open a restaurant. The chef had cooked all over the area and was looking for a new beginning. I talked with him and told him about my love of cooking and my experience with church dinners. He was a bit underwhelmed, so I went back the next day and the next. After about five days he said, "If I give you the job, will you not come back tomorrow?" I agreed and began my career as a chef. The restaurant opened the week before we were to go on the service trip financed in part by my haircut, so I worked a week and then I was gone for eight days. I returned to find that the owner and the chef had had a fight the night before and she had fired him. She put me in charge because I was the only one in the kitchen for whom English was a first language. I went to my colleagues, Carlos and Joao, two Brazilian men who knew what they were doing and told them I understood the dynamic was not fair and I needed their help. I began my training as a chef with those guys.

Part of dealing with the depression was understanding that what had risen to the surface had been there for a long time. I had plastered over important things for years, intentionally and not so intentionally, and the descending darkness called for a drastic remodeling, much like pulling down the old plaster and lathe on Hill Street. I had to take my life down to the studs, as it were, and figure out what to make of the bones of the house that was my life. Cooking was one of the ways I remembered myself, going back to stirring and learning alongside my mother, to cooking for my college roommate who was willing to buy the groceries if I would prepare them, to church dinners, to fixing Saturday Night Chicken for Ginger. I was a cook. I am a cook. The kitchen was a respite for me: a depression-free zone.

The poetry, which became less morose and more meaningful, and my morning journaling reminded me I was a writer and words were also part of my remembering. I got up each day for a couple of years and let the words come out for three pages. In December 2005 that writing became my blog, *Don't Eat Alone*. I also became associate pastor at First Congregational Church of Hanover UCC alongside my restaurant work, which led me back to youth ministry and reconnected me with my love for young people. When I look back, I see how I ended up as a chef and actually began to write regularly and I don't think it's as simple as God caused everything or even God used the depression to lead me to those things. I was a chef and a writer already at some level. I was a teacher as well, except that I was one who couldn't survive grading papers. To make meaning of our suffering does not mean we have to write a happy ending or sing a song of triumph. To make meaning is to recollect the pieces of our past to show ourselves that it was more than wasted time or gratuitous pain. Perhaps it is to show we lived through it, or at least that chapter of it. Forgiveness, even for ourselves, is not forgetting.

Leonard Cohen wrote a song in which he talks about the cracks in everything: "That's how the light gets in,"[17] he says. In my story, home is where Humpty Dumpty did get put back together again, but the reconstruction is obvious. You can see the seams, the scars, the cracks because little streams of light keep busting through. Healing leaves marks of its own. Like any remodeling, what emerges is not simply a new version of what was there before. Then again, the only way we make meaning

---

17 "Anthem" from his 1992 album, *The Future*, SONY/ATV Music.

is in looking back—remembering, reminding, recollecting. One of the challenges for those of us who are people of faith is not to oversentimentalize God's involvement. Those years in Marshfield were tough ones. If I could go back and live them again without the depression and without what it cost Ginger to live through them with me, I would do it in a heartbeat. But we don't get to relive life that way.

I don't think God brought on the depression, or caused it, or even used it to teach me a lesson or shape me because that is not how I picture God working in our lives. My miracle medicine story notwithstanding, I don't see God as so interventionist. I can remember stories that way should I choose to do so, but that is a choice. Jesus said God sees the sparrow fall, but there is nothing about God catching the poor little bird. One of the implications of the Incarnation is the reality of God's presence, but that does not guarantee rescue or deliverance.

Just as living through the worst of the depression did not mean somehow God intervened, its onset did not mean God abandoned me. In those deepest darkest days I was not alone, though I often felt that way. On Halloween night,[18] or maybe the night after, I had let our Schnauzers out into the front yard one last time before we went to bed. I went out with them because the night breeze coming from the water was cool and pleasant. They sniffed around for a minute and then ran to the fence, barking and jumping. I looked up to see a man standing under the streetlight, seemingly out of nowhere. He was in his late seventies, I suppose, wearing a white shirt, a dark suit, and a London Fog topcoat; he had an extra pair of khaki pants rolled up under his arm.

"Good evening," I said. "May I help you?"

---

18 A version of this story was previously published as "Getting Home" in *The Blue Rock Review*, vol. 1, no. 1, 130–33. ©2005 Blue Rock Press, Wimberley, Texas. Used by permission.

"I can't find my car," he answered and laughed as though he was embarrassed.

"Where did you leave it?" The question seemed difficult for him. He looked around, befuddled. I looked closer at him. His face was weathered and kind.

"I need to find Marion Street."

I didn't know where that was. He didn't know where he was. He kept looking around as if he was trying to find his bearings, or hoping to see something familiar.

"What street is this?" he asked.

"This is Bay Street. You're in Green Harbor." I stepped a little closer. "Would you tell me your name?" I asked.

"Yes," he said. "I'm Jack O'Sullivan."

"Wait here, please, Mr. O'Sullivan. I'm going to go inside to see if I can find your address." I went back in the house and told Ginger what was going on. She looked up his name in the Marshfield phone book and found an address that was a few blocks away. She dialed the number as I went back outside.

"The phone book says you live on Canal Street," I told him, "just around the corner."

"We used to live there. Now we live on Marion Street. That's what I need to find."

"My wife is calling to get us some help to find Marion Street," I said. "I'll wait here with you, if that's okay." I wondered what hope Marion Street held for him. I began trying to make conversation, both to pass the time and to see if we might stumble on to some breadcrumb of information that would make the tumblers of his mind fall back into place and unlock his memory. Ginger came out to tell me no one had answered at the number; she had left a message. Though he was lost, no one knew Mr. O'Sullivan needed to be found. Ginger went back inside to call the police. I turned and asked him if he had grown up in Marshfield.

"No," he said. "I grew up in East Boston. We lived on Brinkley Street." For the next several minutes he told me stories of life as a kid in the city and seemed to find some relief in those details that reminded him that he once knew how to get home.

The police cruiser pulled up and a young officer got out. I explained what had happened and, even as I was talking, Mr. O'Sullivan opened the back door to the car and began getting in, saying, "Thank you, thank you" over and over. After I recounted our conversation to the officer, he turned to the old man and asked where he lived.

"On Brinkley Street," he said. My heart sank. His mind had swept away the breadcrumbs that might have shown the way home, leaving him at the mercy of strangers under a streetlight.

"That's okay," said the cop. "We'll get you home."

I walked back inside to hear Patty Griffin singing, "If you break down, I'll drive out and find you; if you forget my love, I'll try to remind you. . . ."[19] I fell back on the couch with Ginger and the pups in the place that held me like home. What helped me feel that way were tactile things: I cooked, I wrote, I gardened, we walked, we talked, we planted trees in the front yard and vegetables in the back. Neither God nor Ginger abandoned me, for which I am eternally grateful, and it was often Ginger's words and Ginger's touch that made God's presence most palpable.

The lie of depression is the isolation: I am the only one in the dark, I am the only one who feels this way, I am the only one who cares about me, I am the only one. The world gets smaller and more claustrophobic, the darkness gets heavier and more relentless, everyone is gone. I can remember only darkness and expect only darkness. Life is the bottomless present. The truth is home is the place you go when there is nowhere else to go.

---

19 Patty Griffin, "When It Don't Come Easy," *The Impossible Dream*, ATO Records, 2004.

Home is the people to whom you go; home is also found in the ones who will come out and find you when you don't show up. Bay Street housed my deepest darkness and one of my brightest lights because, alongside of the depression, that was the place where cooking and writing took hold of me. In the same way I can see the strands of depression back down the years, I can also see how cooking and writing have been in my blood since I was small.

I don't mean to sentimentalize the depression. I would love to live life without it. Though I feel good about how I have learned to live with and through the darkness, the pain has been real, particularly for Ginger. I have said many times over the years that I think it can be harder on the person living with the depressed one than it is on the person who is depressed. Our stories, however, are never monochrome. When I work on a cookie recipe, I have come to say I want the flavors to tell a story: I want there to be a beginning, a middle, and an end. Life has its flavors as well, its layers, as Stanley Kunitz says[20]; we all have several things happening at once. Home is big enough to hold them all.

------

20 "The Layers," www.poetryfoundation.org/poem/242450.

CHAPTER **10**

West Trinity Avenue

these are . . .

the dig in the dirt
go to bed tired
spread out the gravel
plant the trees days

the creak in the knees
crust in the knuckles
come back in five years
to see how it worked out days

the plot the resurrection
slam the door open
say thanks for the help
give thanks for the pups days

the listen to the same riddles
watch him disappear slowly
watch him sit in silence
learn what it means to be family days

the all that I hoped for
never saw it coming
wish there were another way
keep our promises to each other days

the I'm with you
I'm with you
I'm with you
all together now days

W̲E̲ H̲A̲V̲E̲ L̲I̲V̲E̲D̲ in three houses in Durham. The first was a rental house we semi-affectionately dubbed the Summer Camp Cabin, where we waited while our attempt to be nationwide real-estate moguls floundered during the housing crisis a few years back. The second was a wonderful little cottage on Iredell Street in Old West Durham that housed us well until we realized that Ginger's parents needed to move in with us because of her father's Alzheimer's disease. The third, and hopefully the last, is our home on West Trinity Avenue in the downtown neighborhood of Old North Durham.

Family has defined our time in Durham in ways it has not before. We moved to North Carolina in the first place because we wanted to be a day's drive from Birmingham as Ginger's father's illness progressed. Since UCC churches are not plentiful across the South and Ginger wanted to go to a congregation with whom she felt she matched, Durham was as close as we could get. We both have a good sense of family connections, but this was the first time geography played a part in where we chose to live and work. When her parents moved in, I also stopped doing restaurant work because I could not keep that schedule and be who I wanted to be for our family.

From the time we walked into the house on Trinity, it felt more like home—like us—than the other two. Something about the space, the bones, and the stories that had soaked into the walls gave us a sense of belonging, a resonance with all that had come before. We bought the house from the couple who had renovated it and had lived in it while they were fixing it up. In researching the house they found a woman had owned it in the early 1920s, right after it was built, which was quite unusual for that time. An historical marker with her name, Carolyn Grady, hangs below our porch light. When Helena and Sylvia bought the house, it had been condemned. They brought it back from the dead and created a place for us to tell a new story.

For the first time in my life, I moved to make room for my family. We moved to Trinity Avenue to make a home for those we love, those who left their home of forty-five years and the city where they had lived their entire lives because of the insidious disease that was erasing my father-in-law's mind one swipe at a time. In all my moves, this was the first time I moved to make room, to make a place for someone. We had no idea what would happen other than that his Alzheimer's would progress, but we did know it would happen to us together.

One Sunday, Ginger made a comment in her sermon that caught me off guard. "We must remember," she said, "that grieving is somewhat of a luxury." I am sure my head turned like our Schnauzers when they hear an unusual sound. I had never heard that sentence before, yet it rang with resonance in both my head and heart. She was speaking the kind of deep truth rooted in the wisdom of Ecclesiastes: there is a time for grieving and a time for moving, for doing the task at hand. She went on to say that grieving was also a necessity and I heard yet another of the creative tensions of faith within which we are called to live: the necessity and the luxury of grief. We see it as we come to the Communion table together, where we both remember Christ's death and we feed one another with Christ's body. The grief is as real as the hunger around us; we must attend to both.

In our cross-town move, we found an almost continuous reminder that we were not alone in our sojourning. Friends, church members, those we hired to help us do different things, and even people we didn't know were gracious and helpful in ways that reminded us once again that life is not a solo performance. Our home felt destined to be a place full of hope simply based on all the folks who helped us get there. We stood inside and the house seemed to beg for people to be eating and talking around the table, singing on the porch, or chasing fireflies in the backyard as often as we could arrange it. We moved to make room for Ginger's parents. What we discovered was the call was to make room for more than just our family.

Now, here we are: married ministers who live on Trinity Avenue. The poetry of that sentence is significant. However we think about the theological implications of a triune God, the concept of the Trinity means that community and relationship are at the heart of who God is (who God are?). In one of my seminary classes we were discussing Moses's call to go to Pharaoh and demand freedom for the Hebrew people. The reluctant liberator asked, "Whom shall I say sent me?" The King James Version, which was what we used in those days, translated God's reply as, "I am that I am." I told my professor the verse made God sound a great deal like Popeye. In response, he pointed out that the Hebrew was actually an infinitive: God said, "Tell Pharaoh the verb 'To Be' sent you: the very core of existence." At the core of that being is relationship. To be is to be connected. 1 John 4:8 says, "God is love." To be and to love: two inextricable sides to the coin of existence. To be created in God's image is to live life in community, in relationship; remember both life and faith are team sports.

Life in a resurgent downtown neighborhood means living in the middle of a multivoiced conversation that ranges from what will happen to the old warehouses a few blocks over to what has been left on the curb for people to repurpose; from how we get the landlords to make the substandard apartments down the block livable for the residents without pricing them out to what is good at our local restaurants. We are not hoping for a gentrified homogeneous enclave; the variety and diversity are crucial to who we have been and what we hope to become.

What has become the signature event of our life on Trinity Avenue is Thursday Night Dinner. The tradition is not new. It goes back to the early days of our marriage on Hill Street. From the beginning we made place cards for each person around the table, and we have saved them. Once you have a card, you have a place at the table. All we ask is that you let us know you are coming before Wednesday noon so we will have enough food. In our years here on Trinity Avenue the dinners have taken on a new life. Some of it, I think, is because of Durham. This is a town filled with people for whom being together is a primary value. As I have said often, it is the most encouraging place I have ever lived.

Some of it is our big old house that feels as though it was built with open arms. Most of it has to do with who sits around our table from week to week. Our dream has always been to have an open table where new people can find their way into the circle, and they keep doing that. Alongside that dream, we have a collection of regulars for whom Thursday Night Dinner is as much a part of their lives as it is ours. We have become chosen family for one another. They come early to help cook, they stay late to wash dishes, and in between we sit around the table and share our weeks and our lives.

We celebrate and grieve together on a weekly basis. John Berger says, "It is on the site of loss that hopes are born."[21] Around our table each week we have become midwives of hope, if you will. When we clear the table and everyone goes on to

---

21 Berger, *And Our Faces*, 91.

whatever tomorrow holds, I feel as though we have helped to give birth to more hope in our world. As each Thursday night comes to an end, I feel that if all I had to show for this week was that I cooked for and ate dinner with my friends around our table, it would be enough. I only wish the table were bigger.

Alongside the housing of our burgeoning Thursday Night Family, we will remember the house on Trinity Avenue as the place where both our fathers died. Ginger's dad was here, my father was in Texas; home has become where the grief lives. The paradox of existence is that whatever comes next will be enhanced by how deeply we live in this moment. When Ginger and I make another move beyond Durham, it will be made better by the way we invest in our lives here. When I accepted a call to pastor a small rural church my last year in college, my father said, "You and I both know you are not going to stay there forever, but unless you live like you are, you will never invest in the lives of the people there." I am here. Now. I am home.

I was fortunate that I was in my fifties when my father died. In the time since then I have known several other folks who have had to face the same grief, except they have been in their twenties and thirties. They will live with the presence of that significant absence much longer than I. What I am learning about grief in these days is not new, only new to me. My father's death and the death of my father-in-law have made a dimension of life visible in ways I could not see before. After Dad died, I wanted to call or write my friends whose fathers had died before mine and say, "I am sorry. I had no idea. I meant well, I just did not understand how it felt." One of the verses from Isaiah that was used to describe the significance of the Incarnation says, "He was acquainted with grief." The shortest verse in the Bible says, simply, "Jesus wept," and he did so because his friend Lazarus had died, and that added a new dimension to Jesus's humanity.

When I was an English teacher, I used a small story called *Flatland* as the introduction to a British literature course. The book was written in the late nineteenth century by Edwin Abbott, who was both a minister and a mathematician. The central character, A. Square, lived in Flatland, a two-dimensional world. He traveled to Pointland, where the lack of dimensions made him feel quite superior. He also traveled to Lineland, where he was both more knowledgeable and quite misunderstood. Then, at the height of feeling as though he was the pinnacle of the known universe, a three-dimensional Sphere entered his world, requiring him to make room for what he did not know and what he had not seen. My father's death added a new dimension to my life. After August 3, 2013, grief became a primary color.

In learning to deal with death in a way I have not before, I also had to come to terms with a definition of home I had not engaged: heaven as home. Though I grew up singing the old gospel songs, and I love them, I have a hard time with songs that sing as though heaven is more home than here. Yes, we came from God and we are going to God, but for these days in between, are we not at home here? How can we call a place home when none of us has ever been there or seen it or knows what to expect? If heaven is home because God is there, then this is home because God is here.

The more days that pass, the more grief becomes part of the fabric of our lives, even as love grows deeper. Love means more and hurts more at the same time, and the two feel woven together. Here is the risk of Thursday Night Dinner: I love my chosen family, which means I am making myself more open to greater grief. I become more intrigued, even puzzled by the idea of heaven being sorrowless and painless. After a lifetime of learning and growing because of pain—making meaning, as we say—I do not know how to understand what the impetus for growth will be in that dimension I cannot yet comprehend.

I have never connected with the singing-for-ten-thousand-years-streets-of-gold picture of heaven because the picture is one of a static eternity. If we are going to be in the presence of God, who is the essence of imagination and the ultimate creative force—the verb "to be"—how can there not be continued creativity, growth, and meaning? And how does growth happen without disquiet and discomfort? Even as I write I am aware that I am struggling to comprehend something I cannot see, even in the thin places. Whatever lies beyond these days will add to my definition of home. Along with being a place to begin, to become, to build the bonds of family and friends, to make meaning, to share and encourage, and to grieve, it will be a place to end this life and see what happens next. It will be a place where there is room at the table and for us to gather, eat together, and sing the songs that have fed us down the years.

Church Street

subtext

it's been hard to write a
book about home and not
quote lyrics because I
have a satchel full of
songs the soundtrack of a
lifetime ready to play
I guess you'll just have to
come over sometime and
listen maybe sing feels
like home to me we're on
our way home where the
music's playing and I
wonder if I'm ever going
to make it home again

W HEN I STARTED WRITING this book, this chapter was not in the manuscript. We were settled in Durham, we loved our house, and I was starting a cookie business. Then life took a turn. One of the consistent choices Ginger and I have made over the course of our life together is when someone says, "Would you talk to us about . . . ?" our answer is, "Yes," because we want to be open to the ways the Spirit might work that are not readily apparent. When a church in Massachusetts wrote and asked that question, it set a process in motion that led to a conversation with First Congregational Church UCC in Guilford, Connecticut, where Ginger is going to copastor.

Guilford sits on Long Island Sound, its roots going back to the Pilgrims. It is a town that knows a good deal about comings and goings. The church was established in 1643. The parsonage was built about the time they signed the Declaration of Independence; both buildings have seen the town change around them. The Sound empties into the Atlantic just north of the Port of New York from where my parents and I set sail almost six decades ago. When I went up to see the town during Ginger's interview process, I drove down from Hartford on Durham Road and then turned left on the Boston Post Road to find the inn where I was staying. The Post Road was first mail route from New York to Boston. There were three prongs to the paths the mail carriers took, which became what we know as interstates 91, 95, and 84. In the beginning they were known as the King's

Highway, which reminds me of several old gospel songs my dad used to sing. Here in this place I did not know I found traces of all I have let in, hints of what I know as home.

Both roads named destinations that matter to me: my two hometowns. Boston is where Ginger and I grew up together; Durham is where we found an unexpected place to belong. It is the most encouraging city I know. As of this writing, I have traveled to Guilford once. I walked through the parsonage and tried to imagine our things in the house, our colors on the wall, and my writing room in part of the old barn. As you read these pages, I live there. I cross the street most every morning to Perk on Church to get my cortado. I don't expect it to be Cocoa Cinnamon, but I think I will find myself welcome there, along with the deli and the meat market, the old-school hardware store, the farm stand, the church sanctuary, and on the mile long walk down to the harbor. We will have had Thursday Night Dinner, but I don't know who will have been at the table.

Part of belonging is grieving, because life involves leaving. We are moving from Trinity Avenue to Church Street, a fairly poetic gesture for a couple of ministers, I suppose. If the Trinity is a model of relationship and community, the church is the expansion of that idea and the present incarnation of the love of Christ in our world—at least that's what we are called to be. As long as there has been a street in Guilford, there has been a church at the end of it, and for the last two hundred and seventy-five years, our house has sat next door. Our house. I have used those words to describe several significant places in my life. I feel as though I have left home and I have come home all in the same motion on more than one occasion, and now that is happening again. Even for someone who has moved almost all of his life, the packing and leaving part gets more difficult with repetition. Though I am grateful for the ties that bind, I will miss, once more, the daily contact that deepens relationships, even as my days fill with new faces and new invitations to see what love looks like in a different setting. May God bless us in our going out and in our coming home.

HOME COOKING

The Recipes

I DON'T KNOW HOW to think about home without thinking about food, so I have included a sample of recipes old and new, most of which are things people ask me to make again and again. These are some of the flavors of home for me these days.

Roasted Asparagus and Poblano Soup

This was a Thursday Night Dinner recipe that has been worth repeating.

> 2 poblano peppers
> 2 sweet white onions
> 2 leeks (white and light green parts only)
> olive oil
> 5 cloves garlic, crushed
> 2 bunches asparagus, trimmed
> ¼ cup Arborio rice
> 4 cups stock (either chicken or vegetable)
> 2 limes, juiced
> salt and pepper

If you have gas burners on your stove, turn the burner on high and put the poblano peppers directly over the flame until they char. Put them in a mixing bowl and cover with plastic wrap. Let them sweat for 10 or 15 minutes. Take them out of the bowl and, using paper towels, wipe the outer skin and char off the peppers. Then pull them open and clean out the seeds from the inside. If you want more heat in your soup, leave some seeds. Try not to wash the peppers to get them clean; this affects the flavor. (If you don't have a gas burner, put them in the oven for about 20 minutes in a small pan covered with foil and then sweat them.)

Peel the onions and cut them in half. Put the flat side of the onion down and cut across the grain, so you get little half-moon slices. Cut the leeks in half and do the same thing. Put about 2 tablespoons of olive oil in a stock pot over medium heat and add the onions, leeks, and garlic. Cover, stirring occasionally, for about 15 minutes, until the onions begin to caramelize. Cut the asparagus into 1- to 2-inch segments and toss with olive oil and then spread out on a baking sheet. Cook in a 350 degree oven for 10 to 12 minutes. Take out of the oven and add them to the stock pot, along with poblanos, the Arborio rice, and the stock. (The rice will make the soup creamy without adding cream.) Bring the mixture to a boil and then lower the heat and let the soup simmer for about a half an hour.

Remove the soup from the heat and add the lime juice. Puree using an immersion blender, or let the soup cool a bit and carefully puree in batches in either a food processor or a blender. When you serve the soup, drizzle some good olive oil over the top.

Minty Carrot and Orange Soup

I first made this as a cold soup when I worked in a restaurant and we were looking for summer dishes. It can be served either hot or cold.

1 sweet onion, finely chopped
3 tablespoons olive oil
2 red bell peppers
4 cups carrots, sliced ⅛ inch thick
4 cups vegetable stock
1½ cups fresh orange juice
2 tablespoons fresh lemon juice
salt and pepper
2 tablespoons fresh mint, chopped

In a stockpot, sweat the onions with the oil for 6 or 8 minutes and then add the peppers and cook until they soften. I like to keep the pot covered to keep in the juices created by the vegetables. Add the carrots and let the mixture continue to cook down until the carrots begin to soften. Add the vegetable stock, bring the whole thing to a boil, and then lower the heat so that the soup simmers for a good 30 minutes at least. It never hurts a soup to cook a little longer. When the carrots are good and soft, turn off the heat and use a hand mixer to puree the soup. (You can also do it in batches with a food processor.)

Add the orange and lemon juices and make sure everything is mixed well. Season to taste. If the soup is too thick, add more orange juice, or—if you think the orange taste is right—a little cold water.

The mint is the final touch. Do a fine chop on the leaves and then use the immersion blender to mix them into the soup. Cool it down before serving. You want it to taste like it just came out of the refrigerator. The easiest way to cool it is to put the soup in several smaller containers.

Autumn Bisque

This one comes from an afternoon during my restaurant days, making the best of what we had around.

½ pound of bacon, cut into small pieces
2 tablespoons olive oil
1 onion, chopped
2 parsnips, peeled and chopped
2 carrots, peeled and chopped
2 Granny Smith apples, peeled, cored, and chopped
1 onion, chopped
1 piece chorizo sausage (or the sausage of your choosing)
4 cups chicken broth
2 cups light cream
salt
pepper
cinnamon
cayenne pepper

Cook the bacon in the bottom of the stock pot you plan to use. Once it has begun to brown, add the olive oil and the onion. When they begin to become translucent, add the rest of the vegetables and the chorizo and cook on medium high heat for about 5 minutes. Add chicken broth and bring to a boil. Continue cooking until the vegetables are nice and soft. Puree the mixture, and add cream. Add seasonings and let the soup simmer for at least a half an hour. I served it with julienned apples on top.

Curried Squash Soup

2 pounds peeled and cut butternut squash
2 large onions, peeled and quartered
2 Granny Smith apples, cored, sliced thin
6 garlic cloves, peeled
½ teaspoon ground cinnamon
¼ teaspoon ground nutmeg
½ teaspoon dried oregano
1 tablespoon curry powder
salt and pepper
⅛ cup olive oil
2 cans coconut milk
2 cups chicken stock

Preheat oven to 375 degrees.

In a large bowl, mix squash, onions, apples, and garlic and toss with dry spices. Pour on olive oil and then place on a baking sheet and roast for 45 to 60 minutes, or until squash is tender and browned. Remove from the oven and set aside until cool enough to handle. Put the mixture in food processor in batches and puree until smooth (add chicken stock if you need to thin it out). Put in large stock pot and add coconut milk and remaining chicken stock; bring to a boil and simmer gently for 10 to 20 minutes.

Taco Salad

When I was growing up, this was what we had for lunch on Saturdays. Comfort food at its best.

1 onion, diced
1 pound ground beef
1 pkg. taco seasoning
1 head iceberg lettuce, shredded
1 can Ranch Style beans, drained*
2 cups cheddar cheese, shredded
1 small bottle Ranch dressing
Fritos corn chips

Sauté the onion with a little bit of oil until tender; add the beef and half of taco seasoning package and cook until done. Drain and let cool.

---

* Ranch Style beans are only available in Texas. I have used kidney beans or Bush's Chili Beans instead with success.

Shred the lettuce and put it in the bottom of large mixing bowl. Layer beef mixture, beans, the other half of taco seasoning, cheese, and toss. Add dressing to your liking and mix well. Just before serving, toss in the Fritos.

If you don't plan to eat the whole salad at once, keep the meat and bean mixture, dressing, lettuce, and Fritos separate from each other until you're ready to serve; then you can make individual servings as you wish.

Grilled Asparagus, Cherry Tomato, and Corn Salad with Basil Vinaigrette

2 bunches of asparagus
olive oil
salt and pepper
2 ears of corn
1 pint cherry tomatoes

The only thing you cook in this salad is the asparagus.

I use my stove top grill pan. Trim the bottoms of the asparagus spears and toss them in a little olive oil and salt and pepper. Get the grill pan hot and then put a single layer on the pan. Grill them for 4 minutes or so, moving them around so they are heated on all sides. You don't want them to get squishy; just cook them long enough to get some grill marks. Set them aside. When they have cooled, cut them into 1-inch segments.

I like to cut on the bias, which means an angled cut, to give them a little flair.

Stand the corn cob on one end and, using a serrated knife, cut the kernels off the cob. (You can save the cobs in the freezer and add them to stocks or soups later.)

Cut the cherry tomatoes in half. Toss everything together in a big bowl and add the basil vinaigrette.

The dressing

6–8 leaves fresh basil, chopped
¼ cup lemon juice
2 tablespoons apple cider vinegar
2 tablespoons honey or brown sugar
pinch of salt
⅓ cup olive oil

Blend together using an immersion blender or a regular blender until mixture is emulsified. You may need to add a little more oil. Pour over salad and serve. You also may not need all of the dressing—your call.

Gigi's Chicken Salad

This salad answers the musical question: what do you do when the person you love wants chicken salad but hates celery and is allergic to onions?

> chicken, cooked and diced
> granny smith apple, diced
> lemon juice
> dried cranberries
> pecans, toasted and rough chopped
> dijon mustard
> mayonnaise
> salt and pepper

I didn't put amounts because I think chicken salad is one of those things best balanced as you go. I will say this, for a couple of pounds of chicken, you won't need more than a tablespoon of mustard and mix it together with the mayonnaise. Don't peel the apple. I pour a tablespoon or two of lemon juice over the apple while I'm getting everything else ready so it doesn't turn brown. To toast the pecans, set the oven at 400 degrees, put the pecan halves in a pie plate, and roast for about 5 minutes. Chop them after they cool.

Pimento Cheese Stuffed Sweet Potatoes

This was one of my Thanksgiving creations a couple of years ago.

3 large sweet potatoes, wrapped in foil

Preheat oven to 375 degrees. Place sweet potatoes on a baking sheet and then in the oven. Bake for 1 hour, until they feel soft to the touch. Set aside.,

2 cups grated sharp cheddar cheese
½ cup goat cheese
1 small jar pimentos
1 teaspoon bourbon
black pepper
Ritz crackers, crumbled in food processor

Mix the ingredients together except for the crackers. Cut the potatoes in half and scoop them out into a bowl, leaving enough in the skins for them to hold their shape. Combine the pimento cheese mixture with the potato. Put the filling back into the skins and place them side by side in a baking dish. Cover the tops with the cracker crumbs. Lower the oven temperature to 350 degrees and cook for 20 minutes.

Pineapple au Gratin

This has become a Thanksgiving tradition at our house.

    ½ cup self-rising flour
    ½ cup sugar
    ½ cup reserved pineapple juice
    1 20 oz. can pineapple chunks, drained
    1 cup cheddar cheese, shredded

Mix flour, sugar, and pineapple juice. Add pineapple chunks and cheddar cheese and pour into a 9 × 9 casserole dish. Cover and bake at 350 degrees for 20 minutes.

    ½ stick of butter, melted
    1 sleeve Ritz crackers
    ¼ cup brown sugar

Mix butter, crackers, and sugar. Remove casserole from oven and spread mixture over the top. Return to oven and cook uncovered for 15 minutes, or until a knife inserted near the center comes out clean.

Chicken Limone

When we lived in Charlestown, this was a regular meal at our house. I found it in a cookbook from one of the North End restaurants. I have since lost the pages from that cookbook, but found a version online that helped me put it back together. The unusual thing about this recipe is the chicken is dredged in flour and then put in an egg wash and then put in the sauté pan—without going back into flour or bread crumbs. It has a crispy, but very light coating.

> 2 eggs
> ¼ cup milk
> 1 cup flour
> salt and pepper
> ½ cup butter (1 stick)
> 1–2 pounds boneless chicken fillets, cut into 3–4 oz. medallions of uniform thickness
> 4 lemons: slice two and juice two, reserving juice
> 1 tablespoon fresh parsley, chopped

Whisk the eggs and milk together. Spread the flour, seasoned with salt and pepper, in a shallow dish. Heat half of the butter in a skillet over medium high heat. While the butter is getting hot, dredge the chicken in the flour, piece by piece, and then dip each one in the egg wash, and then place it into the sauté pan. Cook the chicken about 3 minutes on each side. If they are pounded thin, this will make sure they are cooked through. (You may have to do this in 2 batches in your sauté pan.) Transfer the chicken to a serving platter and keep warm.

Add the remaining butter to the sauté pan and increase the heat. With a wooden spoon or spatula, loosen the particles from the bottom of the pan. Add the lemon juice and the lemon slices and the parsley. Let the sauce reduce until it begins to brown and thicken a bit; pour it over the chicken and serve.

King Ranch Chicken

The recipe handed down to me called for opening several cans. It tasted good, but I went in search of a way to do it from scratch. Here's what I found.

>   3 tablespoons butter
>   2 cloves garlic, finely chopped
>   1 medium onion, diced
>   1 green bell pepper, diced
>   1 cup mushrooms, sliced
>   1 dried ancho chili, chopped fine (or ½ teaspoon chili
>   powder)
>   3 tablespoons flour
>   1 cup chicken stock or broth
>   1 cup buttermilk
>   salt and pepper
>   1 can Ro-tel tomatoes with green chilis
>   1 jar chopped green olives and pimentos

    4 cups cooked, diced chicken
    1 bunch scallions, finely chopped

Melt the butter in a heavy saucepan over medium heat. Add the garlic, onion, pepper, mushroom, and ancho chili and sauté for 5 minutes. Cover the pot to keep in the moisture. Sprinkle in the flour and stir to mix, making a roux. It should look like a thick paste. Add about ¼ cup of the chicken broth, stirring quickly to remove the lumps and then gradually add the rest of the broth and the buttermilk. Puree the mixture with an immersion blender or in a food processor and return to the stove. Continue cooking and stirring occasionally until the sauce has thickened to the consistency of gravy. Don't bring the liquid to a boil; keep it simmering. Add salt and pepper to taste.

When it gets to the consistency you want, add the tomatoes, olives, chicken, and scallions. Remove from heat.

    8–10 corn tortillas
    2 cups chicken broth
    2–3 cups grated cheddar cheese

Slice the tortillas into thin strips and soak them in the chicken broth for 5 minutes to soften. Grease a 9 × 13 baking dish or a 3-quart casserole and ladle just enough sauce to cover the bottom. Take half the tortilla strips and cover the bottom of the dish. Pour half of the chicken mixture over the tortillas and then top with half the cheese. Repeat the procedure to make a second layer. Cook in a 350-degree oven for about 30 minutes, until the cheese is nicely browned and the casserole is bubbly. Serves 6 to 8—allegedly.

Peanut Butter Sriracha Cookies

The idea map for these went something like this: Peanut butter and chili go together in Thai cooking; chocolate and chili go together in Mexican cooking; let's make cookies.

   1 cup (2 sticks) unsalted butter, softened
   1½ cups peanut butter (crunchy or creamy—your choice)
   2 cups brown sugar, packed
   ½ cup Sriracha
   2 eggs
   1 teaspoon vanilla
   2¾ cups flour
   1 teaspoon baking powder
   1½ teaspoons baking soda
   ½ teaspoon salt
   3 12 oz. packages chocolate chips

Preheat oven to 375 degrees.

In a stand mixer, cream the butter and peanut butter, then add the sugar and let the mixer run for 5 to 7 minutes until the mixture is light and fluffy. Add the Sriracha with the mixer on low. Add the eggs, one at a time, and then the vanilla. Beat until well combined.

In a separate bowl, mix the remaining dry ingredients except for the chocolate chips. Gradually add the flour mixture to the peanut butter mixture and then add the chocolate chips. Mix until well combined.

Refrigerate the dough for 1 hour. I used a 1-ounce cookie scoop and then rolled the scoops into balls about an inch in diameter, placed them on a lined baking sheet, and pressed them down gently with a fork.

Bake for 8 to 10 minutes. If you want a bigger cookie, use a 2-ounce scoop and bake them for 11 to 13 minutes.

Elvis Has Left the Building Cookies

Ginger and I were heading out of town for a couple of weeks, which meant I was going to be gone from my job at the computer store, which meant I wouldn't be taking in cookies for a while, which inspired these peanut butter-banana-chocolate chip treats.

  1 cup butter, room temperature
  1 cup peanut butter
  1 banana, mashed
  2 cups brown sugar, firmly packed
  2 eggs
  1 teaspoon banana extract
  3 cups flour
  1 teaspoon baking powder
  1 teaspoon baking soda
  ½ teaspoon salt

1 12 oz. package of semi-sweet chocolate chips
1 cup (generous cup) dried banana chips

Preheat the oven to 375 degrees.

Cream the butters, banana, and sugar together in an electric mixer. As I have said before, I usually let the mixer run 5 to 7 minutes. Then add the eggs and banana extract and mix until combined. In a separate bowl, mix together the remaining dry ingredients except for the chocolate chips and the banana chips. Combine well and then gradually add to the butter-sugar mixture in the electric mixer until everything is incorporated.

Add the chocolate and banana chips and mix it all together well. Use a 1-ounce scoop to drop the cookies on a baking sheet lined with parchment paper. Bake for 12 to 14 minutes. Makes 5 dozen. Thank you. Thank you very much.

Orange-Cranberry-Rosemary Icebox Cookies

An icebox cookie is basically a sugar cookie you chill (in the icebox—er, refrigerator) and then slice before cooking.

    1 cup butter, room temperature
    2 cups brown sugar
    2 large eggs
    1 2-ounce bottle of orange extract
    1 cup dried cranberries
    a big handful of finely chopped fresh rosemary.
    3½ cups flour
    ½ teaspoon baking soda
    ½ teaspoon salt
    3 tablespoons orange zest or dried orange peel

Beat the butter and sugar together in a stand mixer for 5 to 7 minutes. Add eggs and vanilla and beat until well combined.

Put cranberries and rosemary, along with a half a cup of flour in the food processor and pulse 3 or 4 times. Add to the rest of the flour and then combine with the baking soda, salt, and zest together in a separate bowl. Add flour mixture gradually to butter mixture.

Divide dough into 4 equal parts and form each section into a log about 1½ to 2 inches in circumference. Chill for at least 2 hours. The dough will keep for up to 3 days in the fridge. You can also freeze it. When you're ready to cook, preheat the oven to 350 degrees. Line your baking sheet with parchment paper. Slice the dough into ¼ inch slices and place them on the baking sheet. I find I can cook 18 on sheet at a time. Bake 8 to 9 minutes. Makes 8 to 10 dozen cookies.

Lemon-Basil-Ginger Cookies

My search for a summertime cookie led me to this..

    ¾ cup butter, room temperature
    ¾ cup sugar
    1 large egg
    1 tablespoon lemon zest
    1 2-ounce bottle lemon extract
    ½ cup crystallized ginger, chopped fine
    ⅓ cup fresh basil, julienned
    2 cups flour
    ½ teaspoon baking powder
    ¼ teaspoon salt
    ½ cup sugar (for rolling cookes)

Preheat oven to 350 degrees.

Cream butter and sugar for 5 to 7 minutes. Add the egg and beat until mixed well. Add the next 3 ingredients and mix until everything is combined.

Put the julienned basil in a food processor with about ½ cup of flour and pulse it into fine pieces. Whisk it in with the rest of the flour in a separate bowl from the butter mixture and add the other dry ingredients. Add to the butter mixture a little bit at a time, mixing until combined.

Using a 1-ounce cookie scoop, drop the cookies into the sugar and roll until they are covered. Put them on a cookie sheet and press them down lightly with your hand. Bake for 12 minutes. Makes about 3 dozen.

Cocoa Cinnamon Treats

The story behind these cookies begins with a request from one of my colleagues for a sugar cookie with either chocolate chips or toffee. I thought, "Why not both?" The first incarnation was pretty good, but I had some ideas on improvements. Our friends Areli and Leon opened a coffee shop in our neighborhood called Cocoa Cinnamon, so, with them in mind, I made a version rolled in sugar mixed with both cocoa powder and cinnamon, along with a touch of cayenne pepper. These may be the best cookies I have ever made.

> ½ cup butter, room temperature
> ½ cup shortening
> 1 cup packed brown sugar
> ¼ cup white sugar
> 1 egg
> 1 teaspoon vanilla extract
> 2 cups all-purpose flour

1 teaspoon baking soda
½ teaspoon baking powder
¼ teaspoon salt
1 tablespoon instant espresso powder
1 12 oz package semi-sweet chocolate chips
1 (6 ounce) package Heath Bits O' Brickle chips
1 cup white sugar
1 teaspoon cocoa powder
1 teaspoon cinnamon
½ teaspoon cayenne pepper

Preheat oven to 350 degrees.

Mix the butter, shortening, and sugars for 5 to 7 minutes. Add the egg and vanilla and mix until blended.

In a separate bowl mix flour, baking soda, baking powder, salt, and espresso powder until blended. With the mixer on low, add incrementally to the butter mixture until combined. Add chocolate chips and toffee bits and mix until combined. In another bowl, mix sugar, cocoa powder, cinnamon, and cayenne pepper and set aside. This is to coat the cookies.

Using a 1-ounce scoop, drop balls of the dough into the cocoa-cinnamon mixture and roll them to coat. Put them on a cookie sheet lined with parchment paper and bake for 9 to 10 minutes. I choose the lesser time because it makes a wonderfully soft cookie.

Milton's Ginger Cookies

Here's how the story goes: In Asian cooking, ginger and chilis go together, so I decided to add some cayenne pepper alongside of everything else. Then I thought about the chili and chocolate combination in Mexican cooking and added a little cocoa powder. The result is one seriously good cookie.

1½ cups butter (at room temperature)
2 cups brown sugar
½ cup molasses
2 eggs
4 cups flour
1 tablespoon and 1 teaspoon baking soda
½ teaspoon salt
¼ teaspoon ground cloves
2 teaspoons ground cinnamon
3 teaspoons ground ginger
1 teaspoon cocoa powder
½ teaspoon cayenne pepper

Preheat the oven to 375 degrees.

Mix the butter, brown sugar, and molasses in a stand mixer for 5 to 7 minutes. Add eggs and mix until well combined.

In a separate bowl, mix the remaining ingredients and add the dry mixture gradually to the butter-sugar mixture. Use a 1-ounce scoop and roll them in sugar before putting them on the baking sheet. Cook for 11 to 13 minutes. I cook my 1-ounce cookies for 11; if I use a 2-ounce scoop, I cook them for 13.